15°

D1106748

TRADE
WINDS

ahu

MOLOKAI

Battle of the
Damming of the Waters

LANAI

x

MAUI

KAHOOLAWE

Battle of the
x Red-mouthed Guns

Kawaihae

MAUNA
KEA

Kailua

HAWAII

Hilo

Kealakekua
Bay

KILAUEA

MAUNA
LOA

Hawaii's
First
King

Hawaii's First King

by James T. Pole

the NEW *Bobbs-Merrill* COMPANY, INC.

AN ASSOCIATE OF HOWARD W. SAMS & CO., INC.

Publishers • INDIANAPOLIS • NEW YORK

Copyright © 1959 by The Bobbs-Merrill Company, Inc.

Printed in The United States of America

First Edition

Library of Congress Catalog Card Number: 59-14297

Contents

Foreword

IN THE CENTER of a cluster of government
buildings in Honolulu stands a majestic brown and gold statue.
The erect noble figure holds a spear in his left hand and ex-
tends his right arm in a gesture of regal benevolence. A golden-
crested helmet shines on his head, and a golden cloak, open at
the front, reaches from his shoulders to the ground.

He is Kamehameha the Great, the warrior king who conquered and united the Hawaiian Islands. Kamehameha was a
wise and able leader of men who lived a most eventful and
inspiring life against the brilliantly romantic background of
old Hawaii. During his active lifetime he earned the right to
a place among those builders of nations who truly deserve to be
called "the Great." He skillfully guided his people from the
stagnant doldrums of barbarism into the warm current of
civilization and progress.

After Kamehameha's death, native historians and the missionaries who taught them to write collected the facts and
traditions of his reign. But for a vivid firsthand portrait of the
builder of Hawaii one must go to the salty journals of men who

sailed the seas and stopped during his lifetime at his green and friendly islands. Explorers like Captain Cook and George Vancouver knew Kamehameha and wrote about him. Adventurers, merchant skippers, and foreigners who settled in his kingdom to work for him all kept their journals.

These writings of the first Americans and Europeans to know the islands are preserved in the libraries of Hawaii, and this story of Kamehameha is drawn from their yellowed pages.

The Hawaiian names may look odd to you because of their liberal use of vowels, but those are the sounds that give the language its liquid, musical quality. Every syllable is either a vowel alone, or a consonant plus a vowel. The next to the last syllable is accented.

Pronounce each vowel separately, except for the combinations *ai* (*ai*sle), *ei* (r*ei*gn), *oi* (*oi*l), *au* (n*ow*). And give the vowels their Continental values: *a* (f*a*ther), *e* (s*a*y), *i* (s*ee*), *o* (*o*pen), *u* (s*oo*n). So many of the names begin with *Ka* or *Ke* or *Ku,* which represent the definite article *the,* because they are descriptive. For example, Ka-meha-meha means "The Lonely One," or "The One Set Apart."

Hawaii's

First

King

CHAPTER I

A Stone Is Overturned

On a wild, stormy night in November 1753, Alapai the Great, king of Hawaii, was encamped on the northern tip of his island. His army was poised for one more attempt to conquer the neighboring island of Maui. The wind drove level sheets of rain through the camp and hurled along huge fronds wrenched from the palm trees. Flashes of lightning tore the sky open with ear-splitting cracks.

In and out of Alapai's grass hut scurried a steady stream of chiefs and messengers carrying reports of damage and orders for protecting the army's canoes and equipment. One warrior, who was evidently the bearer of bad news, threw himself trembling at the king's feet.

"Well," demanded Alapai, "what is it?"

The man rattled out his message all in one breath, as though to get a bad thing over quickly.

"The child has been born but they have sent it away."

Alapai jumped to his feet.

11

"What!" he shouted. "Who told you this?"

"I know it myself, O king. I saw your niece, and her child had been born. But when we got there it had been taken away."

"Was it a boy?" the king demanded.

"Yes, your Majesty."

"Get out and find it!" roared Alapai, and his voice was husky with rage. "Search the camp and the forest paths. Find it and do as I ordered."

When the man had gone, Alapai waved his gaping warriors out of the hut and sat down on a pile of mats. Yes, he thought, I have been too softhearted. I should have taken no chances. The girl should have been killed long before her child was born. Or was it useless, after all, to tamper with the plans of the gods?

About a year earlier a young chief had fallen in love with a niece of King Alapai and married her. Some time later the young bride had set the court agog with a most unusual request. She wanted a certain one of the chiefs to be put to death so that she might have his eyeballs!

Now Alapai was not easily shocked or particularly squeamish—he always took on his expeditions a wooden platter on which he cut up the flesh of conquered chiefs for shark bait—but this demand of his niece's was certainly out of the ordinary. There must be something behind it.

He summoned an old *kahuna* who had been famous for years as a soothsayer and asked him to interpret his niece's morbid wish.

"It is a clear sign from the gods," the old priest told him.

"Your niece will bear a child. A man is coming who will slay the chiefs."

The king was not satisfied and called in other *kahunas*. Their interpretation was the same: "A rebel is coming, a man who will slay the chiefs."

Alapai was now genuinely alarmed. The warning was too strong to be taken lightly. Rebels had never been welcome in Alapai's domain, and he himself was quite capable of handling any slaying of chiefs that needed to be done.

"We will pluck the bud," he announced, smiling grimly, "lest it grow and spread." And he bound the soothsayers, on pain of death, to say nothing of what had passed.

But one of the priests was willing to risk his life. Why, he asked himself, should his words cause the death of a still-unborn child? And did even the king have the right to set himself up against the will of the almighty gods? The priest went to Keoua, the girl's husband, and told him what the king had said.

Keoua was thrilled by the words of the prophecy. To him it meant that the child his wife was going to give him would one day be a great king, undoubtedly the ruler of all Hawaii. With the help of his brother, Kalaniopuu, he laid careful plans to preserve the child from the cruelty of Alapai.

And so, on that night in November, while the tempest lashed the Kohala coast, the baby was born. His first lusty cry was nearly drowned out by the noise of the storm. The midwife hurriedly wrapped the infant in folds of tapa cloth and handed him to Naeole, one of Kalaniopuu's runners. By the time the king's men got word of what had happened, the son of Keoua was being carried swiftly through the dripping forests.

The place selected for hiding the child was Awini, a lonely village in the mountains of Hamakua. It was governed by an old mountain chief, and his granddaughter was to be the baby's

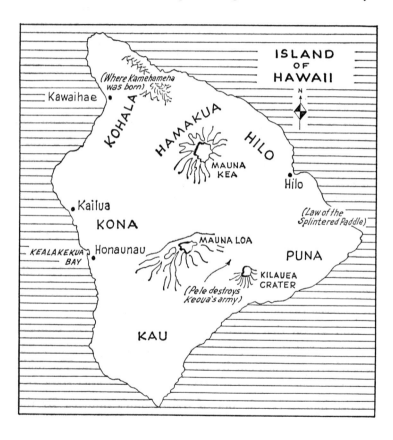

nurse. For weeks she and her mother had been getting ready for their precious charge. The two women had already started work on the feather cloak he would wear as a chief. In one corner of the hut lay a pile of *olona* fibers for weaving the net on which the brilliant red and yellow feathers would be fastened.

Hardly had the women taken the warm, rain-soaked bundle from Naeole and begun to unwrap it, than there was a warning shout from outside. The old chief standing guard had heard runners coming along the trail. The women thrust the baby under the pile of *olona* fibers and prayed that it would not cry. Naeole ran out and hid behind the house.

A minute later a party of Alapai's henchmen, who were already scouring the countryside, peered in at the door.

"Have you seen a man with a bundle pass this way?" one of them asked. "A man carrying a child?"

The women's hearts were pounding in their throats, but the girl forced herself to answer calmly. "No," she said, "we have seen no one. Who would come here on a night like this?"

There was no sound from the pile of fibers in the corner. The men grunted and passed on down the jungle trail.

The next day Keoua visited the mountain hideaway.

"Naeole," he said to the runner who had carried the child there, "my son is to stay here with this family until I can send for him. He will be safe here. I want you to remain with him as his *kahu* and teach him all you know."

The chubby brown baby was given the pet name of Paiea, "The Soft-shelled Crab." For twelve years he was cared for by the mountain chieftain Umi and his devoted family. There was almost no contact with the outside world, for King Alapai took little interest in the doings of so tiny and inaccessible a part of his realm as Awini. Keoua occasionally visited his son, but not often enough to arouse suspicion. Sometimes Kalaniopuu came along to see his young nephew.

Those were red-letter days for Paiea when the two tall warriors would appear unannounced at the little settlement. How proud he was when they felt his muscles and asked him to show how far he could throw his javelin. And how his chest swelled when he was told that he was stronger than any of the boys at the royal court. At Awini there were no other boys of his own age, and his only playmate was a little girl, the daughter of his foster mother. He soon outgrew the games she liked to play.

Paiea and his *kahu* Naeole were closer to one another than father and son, for Naeole devoted his whole time to the care and education of his noble charge. He was with the boy always, roaming the forest paths with him through the long day and sleeping by his side at night.

Naeole's purpose was to make the boy an all-round athlete. He taught him wrestling and *mokomoko,* the peculiar Hawaiian straight-arm style of boxing. And with an eye to the future he showed Paiea how to throw javelins and spears, and how to dodge them or snatch them from the air and hurl them back.

The long days out of doors with Naeole were a delight to Paiea, but the evenings were good, too. There would be a dinner to satisfy even the biggest appetite. Chicken or pig or dog baked in a hole with hot stones. Gourd bowls full of poi, the root of the taro plant pounded to a mush and allowed to ferment until it had a buttermilk taste. There were always sweet potatoes and bananas and coconuts, and for dessert perhaps a piece of juicy sugar cane.

Then, before bedtime, the lad would curl up on a mat to listen to tales of monsters and marvels and heroes. Umi and the women knew them by the dozen.

Paiea liked stories of Hawaiian strong men, like the demigod Maui who had held back the sun. When the god's mother complained that she didn't have time enough to do her day's work, he climbed to the top of the volcano Haleakala, "The House of the Sun," and by holding onto its rays forced the sun to travel more slowly.

There were many hair-raising stories of the shark-men who would turn into sharks in the water and attack their unsuspecting companions. And amusing ones about the dwarflike gnomes, the *menehune,* who could build a fish pond or a wall around a field in a single night while everyone was asleep.

While the stories went round, the women worked on Paiea's feather cloak, the one they had started before he was born. It would take years to make, because each mamo bird supplied only two of the golden-yellow feathers, one under each wing. They were woven so closely on the fiber net that the finished material had the texture of deep velvet. Paiea wondered if it could possibly be ready for him by the time he became a chief.

The more serious part of Paiea's schooling was taken care of by Naeole. He described to the boy the beauties and wonders of his homeland and taught him the lore and customs of his people. He pictured for his little pupil the string of islands: Hawaii, like a great fallen comet set in the sea with its tail of smaller islands—Maui, Lanai, Molokai, Kahoolawe, Oahu, Kauai, Niihau.

He taught the boy the names and attributes of the great gods: Kane, the supreme kindly god of nature; Ku, the fierce war god who demanded human sacrifices; Lono, god of the peaceful life; Kanaloa, ruler of the sea.

Naeole held a fanatical belief in the high destiny that the gods had in store for his young pupil. When Paiea was old enough to understand, the faithful *kahu* told him of the prophecy of the soothsayers. And from then on he missed no chance of impressing the boy with the conviction that one day he would be a great king.

Near the town of Hilo there lay a long, flat stone that looked like a fallen monument from some ancient, forgotten time. The legends said that only the boys of a lost race of kings had ever been able to turn the Naha Stone over.

When Paiea was nearly twelve years old, Naeole secretly took him to the place where the stone lay. He had not the slightest doubt that the lad could move it. And he was right. Paiea grasped the edge of the slab and heaved, and over it went.

A shriveled old priestess who lived near the place had come up to watch. When she saw how easily Paiea had moved the stone she went down on her knees before him.

"I will make a prophecy," she said, "one that will certainly come true. This boy will grow up to be an overturner of thrones, just as he has overturned the Naha Stone. He will be the ruler of a larger empire than has ever been known in these islands."

Naeole too kneeled down in reverence.

"Paiea," he said, "I have taught you the religious prohibitions, the tabus. You know it is death for a commoner to remain standing in the presence of a chief. You know it is death to remain standing when the king's drinking water is being carried past. It is death for a woman to enter a temple, or to go into the eating house of men, or to eat the tabu foods—pork, bananas, coconuts."

"Yes," Paiea broke in, "you have told me all the things that must not be done, but you have not told me *why* they must not be done."

"I will tell you now," said Naeole, "for now you are old enough to understand. The tabus may cause much discomfort, but they are really in the interest of all. The chiefs and priests, and especially the king, must be kept apart from everything common or corrupt, for it is through them that mana flows from the gods to the entire nation. Mana is the soul of the universe, a sort of spiritual energy without which no man or nation can be great.

"Each man acquires an original supply of mana from the social rank into which he happens to be born. He can increase it by prayer, by strict observance of the tabus and the homage due to the gods, and by the success of his everyday life. He can decrease it, on the other hand, by neglect of these things. Which will you do?"

Paiea listened with a thoughtful, unsmiling face. He stepped up to Naeole and placed his hand on the man's shoulder.

"I know that my inherited mana is great," he said. "I will add to it by living as you have taught me. I will revere the gods and perform noble deeds. If the gods want me to be a king, I will be a great one. I will be a king more powerful than any in the stories old Umi has told me."

CHAPTER 2

Into the Ring

On Paiea's twelfth birthday Naeole gave him wonderful news. He was to go to the court of King Alapai. One of his father's runners had arrived only that morning.

The boy was so excited that he hardly knew which question to ask first. He loved old Umi and the rest of the family as though they were his own flesh and blood. Of course he would be sorry to leave them. But to live at court! To see the great crowds of people and mingle with famous warriors! And there would be the sea, the canoe trips and fishing and surf riding that were impossible at Awini. Here he was forced to be content with learning to swim and dive in a cold pool at the foot of a mountain waterfall.

Suddenly a new thought came into his mind. He turned to Naeole with a look of concern.

"Are you going to live with me at the court?" he asked.

"If you want me to, Paiea," answered his tutor. "Your

father has asked me to go with you and continue to be your *kahu*."

"Then I will go," decided Paiea solemnly.

Naeole was relieved and glad when he got the message from Keoua. It was not right that the boy should be penned any longer in these lonely mountains. He would turn into a hermit. It was time he went to live in the surroundings that were rightfully his, and he needed the companionship of boys his own age. The *kahu* had noticed this past year how restless Paiea was at times and had wondered how much longer he would be able to hold the lad at Awini.

The very next morning, after long, tearful embraces and prayers by his foster family that the gods would protect him, Paiea turned his back on the only home he had ever known. He and Naeole set out westward toward the Kohala coast.

The first part of the journey was along narrow paths that wound among the tall koa trees and giant ferns of the forest, cool and silent save for the twittering of innumerable birds. In the middle of the afternoon the travelers came out into an open upland of neat sweet potato and taro plantations. And there in the distance, about three hours' walk away, lay the royal town of Kawaihae, "The Raging Surf," spread out along the shore of the sea.

It was a hot, dusty tramp across this unshaded farm country, and, by the time they entered the town, Paica was very tired. But he was determined not to show it. He strode bravely along with his head high, past the sharp-peaked grass houses that stood in little family groups in their low-walled enclosures. He had never before seen so many people. Men and women were at work in their yards, pounding taro root for poi or making tapa cloth. Others were just loafing in the shade. Pigs, dogs, chickens, and naked brown children were everywhere.

Keoua met his son and took him straight to the king's house. Before Paiea prostrated himself beside his father he had a glimpse of a grim, wrinkled face, white-bearded and lean.

Alapai had been reminded of the existence of Paiea by hearing him named in a poem—one of the long, tedious kind made up mostly of recitals of family trees. The king lifted his head at the name and broke in on the bard:

"Paiea? Paiea, the son of Keoua? Ah, yes. I remember. Keoua, where is the boy now?"

Keoua had known for some time that the king's fear of the prophecy had died away. But he had thought it best to wait for an opportunity such as this one.

"He lives in the mountains, your Majesty."

Alapai was in a good mood. "In the mountains? Are you trying to make a woodchopper out of him? Bring him here to the court where he belongs."

Now the king spoke to the boy lying prone in homage before him:

"Stand up, Paiea, and let us see what you look like."

Alapai peered approvingly at the proud, erect young figure with its solemn face and well-developed limbs.

"I have decided that you shall live here and learn how to be a warrior," he said in a kindly tone. "Will you like that?"

"Yes, your Majesty," answered Paiea.

"Good. Kekuhaupio there shall be your tutor." The king nodded toward a bearded, middle-aged warrior. "See that you pay attention to him, and one day you shall be an officer in my army."

"But, your Majesty," Paiea blurted out quickly in a distressed voice, "I already have a *kahu*. Naeole came with me from Awini."

Alapai liked the lad's display of spirit and loyalty.

"Your Naeole will do well enough to teach you how to swim, and you shall keep him," he said. "But Kekuhaupio will be a better battle tutor. Now go along with your father."

Keoua turned toward the door, but Paiea did not move.

"Well," asked Alapai, "what now?"

"Your Majesty," answered the boy, "I wish no longer to be called Paiea. It is a child's name. Now that I am to become a warrior I wish to be called Kamehameha."

There was something in the earnest tone and the intense young face that prevented the king from laughing. It was impossible not to take the request seriously.

"Kamehameha, eh?" said Alapai. "It is a good name. There have been great warriors in these islands who have borne it. What does it mean in your case, 'The Very Lonely One'? Or perhaps, 'The One Set Apart'? Well, Kamehameha it shall be."

Both of Alapai's translations of the name were highly appropriate to the boy. His life thus far had certainly been a lonely one, and already he looked upon himself as one set apart for future greatness.

Now the young prince began a long course of training for the time when he would come of age and take his place as a high chief of Hawaii. Women had no further part in his upbringing: all that had been left behind at Awini. His studies now were manly sports and the art of warfare, and he soon proved himself an apt pupil. Kekuhaupio taught him how to handle his weapons skillfully. He also taught him the tactics and strategy of the battlefield and how to lead and inspire men.

It was one of the proudest days of Kamehameha's youth when he was put through the ceremony that made him a fully qualified fisherman. Fish was one of the three Hawaiian staffs of life—the other two were pork and poi—and the sea around the islands teemed with dozens of varieties. Because fish was such a staple food, the catching of it was governed by solemn rituals and tabus, and one of the most important was the initiation of the new fisherman.

For weeks before the ceremony Kamehameha had studied and practiced all the various ways of catching fish. He went with fishing parties far out to sea after swordfish that weighed three or four hundred pounds, and aku, the giant striped tuna. He learned how to throw the big circular nets accurately and how to use the harpoon and fish spear.

He learned, too, strange methods that had been used since ancient times. How to spread on the shallow reef water the ground-up pods of the fish poison tree so that the fish became drugged and could be scooped up. And how to lay a rope of twisted banana leaves in a circle on the water so that it would cast a shadow through which the fish were afraid to pass.

At last Kamehameha was declared ready for the initiation. He must speak to no one on the way to the fishing canoe. Once at sea, he was not allowed to cast his line until the other fishermen had completed their day's catch. Then he was told to catch one fish. Within a few minutes he had hooked a beautiful striped tuna that weighed nearly seventy pounds. When the party got back to the beach a *kahuna* cut up the fish and baked it. The men who had taken Kamehameha out all ate pieces of it, murmuring prayers for his continued success. To complete the ceremony, the young prince wrapped all the bones in large green leaves and threw them into the sea. He was now a fully qualified fisherman.

Probably no other sport gives a man the feeling of being as much a part of the force and movement of nature as does surfboard riding. As Kamehameha learned it at Kawaihae Bay, with its rock-fringed shoreline, it was a reckless and dangerous competitive sport. It called forth all the skill and courage and co-ordination of the trained athlete.

The riders who were going to race back to the beach must first of all get their smooth, oiled boards out beyond the breakers, the white beards of the sea gods. Lying prone, they paddled the boards along with their hands, gliding over the small smooth waves and ducking under the high foaming ones. Then, half a mile from the shore, they lined up sitting astride their boards to wait for a large wave. When they saw it coming they stretched out on their boards again and began paddling toward the beach with all their strength. As the wave caught them and lifted them up, they must distribute their weight just right or they would be out of the race at the very start. The board would either slide off the back of the wave or plunge helplessly down its face to the jagged coral shelf below.

But those who got themselves successfully launched still had the greatest danger ahead of them. Kneeling or standing on their boards, they would be hurtled along at racehorse speed toward the line of black boulders. Those who failed to steer between them were forced to jump disgracefully off and leave their precious boards to be dashed to pieces against the rocks. The first man to shoot up onto the beach won the race.

Kamehameha became such an enthusiastic and skillful follower of this Hawaiian sport of kings that even in his old age he was known as one of the most expert surf riders in the islands.

Kamehameha got his first taste of actual fighting when he was seventeen years old.

King Alapai died, and the throne was claimed by a son of the king and by Kamehameha's uncle, Kalaniopuu. Kamehameha's father had died a year or so earlier. The young chief joined the forces of his uncle and took part in a battle near

Kealakekua Bay in which the army of the other contender was defeated. He had helped to make a king, and he had begun his career as a warrior.

From this time until he was over forty, Kamehameha was almost constantly in battle. For no sooner had Kalaniopuu become king than he found a brand-new excuse to take up the old contest with Maui.

His son Kiwalao had married the only child and heiress of the Maui king. Now came news that the king was dead and that the throne had been seized by the dead king's brother, Kahekili the Thunderer, a man who was to be the arch enemy of Hawaii for many long years to come.

"He is a usurper!" cried Kalaniopuu. "I will not rest until I have secured for my son the inheritance that is rightfully his."

And he spent the remaining ten years of his life in one unsuccessful attempt after another to make good his vow.

The most important result of these years of fighting was the rise of Kamehameha to a generalship in the Hawaiian army before he was twenty-five. Kekuhaupio had done his work well. And that doughty warrior felt amply repaid when in one of the battles his pupil saved him from being impaled on a spear hurled by Kahekili himself. Kamehameha snatched it from the air just as it was about to pierce the body of his battle tutor.

Such fame did Kamehameha win in these campaigns that a bard composed a chant in his honor and sang it at court. In stirring masculine phrases the poet celebrated the young chief's prowess and foretold his future glory:

Soon, behold the shadow of one seizing the land,
  Even the son of Keoua;
The youth doing the work of the chief,
  Wrestling for the islands.
Boldly stepping into the ring, he advances with
  Right-handed and left-handed blows;
He curbs the islands with a strong hand.

CHAPTER 3

Gods on Floating Islands

THE YOUNG GENERAL Kamehameha received
an urgent summons to attend a council at his uncle's headquarters that had been set up in the invasion camp on the
island of Maui. When he entered the building and took his
place, most of the high chiefs and priests who had accompanied the army to Maui were already ranged along the sides
of the room.

King Kalaniopuu was sitting on his throne, a pile of *lauhala*
mats. On either side of him a servant lazily waved a bright
feather fly chaser. Within easy reach sat the bearer of the royal
spitbox, ready to present it whenever the king turned his head.
A chief's spittle must be disposed of with great care, of course,
lest an enemy *kahuna* use it to work harmful sorcery. Especially here on Maui must one be on his guard. The crafty
Kahekili missed no tricks.

It was late in November of 1778, and Kalaniopuu, having
added two Maui provinces to his domain, was about ready to

return to Hawaii for the *makahiki* season. No man fought or worked then, but spent the long holiday in a round of sports and merrymaking in honor of the god Lono. And this might turn out to be the most memorable *makahiki* festival in the history of Hawaii.

Could such a miracle be possible as the thing Kalaniopuu's scouts had reported only this morning? One man alone could not know what to think. He must have the opinions of his wisest *kahunas* and chiefs, for the scouts had brought word that the god Lono himself, riding the sea on two marvelous floating islands, was approaching the land!

Kalaniopuu ordered the scouts brought in to retell their strange tale. They were plain fighting men, the two of them, very self-important at finding themselves the center of so much attention. Some listeners had believed them; others had called them liars. But they knew what they had seen and were sticking to their story.

Their patrol had crept up along the east coast of Maui, said the older scout, well into enemy territory. Just about dawn yesterday morning, while they were making breakfast among the trees, they heard wild shouts from a near-by village. They looked where all the people were pointing, and could not believe their eyes. Far out to sea, sharply outlined against the morning sky, were two floating islands, the islands of Lono.

Kamehameha broke in on the speaker impatiently. "Why do you call them islands? Do you mean to tell us you have seen stones and earth floating on the sea?"

"No, O chief," the man replied. "They looked to be all

wood and they had steep sides. But there were three tall trees on each one, trees with many branches."

"Were leaves growing on the trees?"

"No, they had no leaves. But great white banners were hanging on them—the *makahiki* banners of Lono."

"He-a!" exclaimed Kamehameha with unbelieving disgust. But before he could go on, Kalaniopuu spoke in a kindly tone. He could see the men were frightened by his nephew's bluntness.

"Did you go out to the—er—'floating islands'?"

"No, your Majesty. We were afraid to go among the people of the village. But last night when it was dark we stopped a man. He had been on them. He said the men on them were gods, volcanoes, for fire burns in their mouths. They have loose skin with openings in the sides where they keep their belongings. He said these gods speak a strange language among themselves."

Up to now the younger scout had said nothing, but this was his cue to tell what had struck him funniest of all.

"Your Majesty," he broke in, "this is the way the man said the gods speak: 'A hikapalale, hikapalale, hioluai, oalaki, poha walawaki'."

Kalaniopuu dismissed the soldiers.

"Well," he asked his councilors, "what do you make of this?"

Kamehameha spoke up. "It is hard to make much of the wild tales of these men. We must see this wonder for ourselves."

There was a murmur of agreement.

"But I believe these are the same people that stopped at Kauai last year. We were told they had white faces and holes in their skin, and that they carried fire in their mouths and their words could not be understood. I think they are foreigners who have come to dwell in the land, and I say let us be on our guard."

"What need to be on guard against the kindly god Lono?" asked a stout priest. "These beings are certainly no foreigners, but gods, and Lono himself will be found among them. He has come back on a floating temple, as he promised centuries ago, to be with us during his *makahiki* festival."

The muttering and nodding of heads as the *kahuna* spoke showed that many of the council agreed with him.

Long ago, according to the legends, Lono, the god of agriculture and all peaceful occupations, had lived on Hawaii at Kealakekua, "The Path of the God." But he quarreled with his wife, whom he really loved very much, and hit her over the head with a stone checkerboard. When he saw her lying bleeding and unconscious, he was so grief-stricken and ashamed that he sailed off across seas. But before going he made a promise: "I will return in later times on an island bearing coconut trees and swine and dogs."

All the chiefs fell silent as Kau, the high priest, leaned forward to speak. He sat erect and bright-eyed in spite of his great age, a white-bearded image of wisdom.

"Kamehameha has spoken wisely," he said. "We must see these visitors before we can know who they are. If this is indeed Lono, he will surely reveal himself. But let us remember that not for many centuries have the heavenly gods walked in this lower world. I recall the words of a great seer. 'Some day,' he prophesied, 'foreigners will come here, white people. And as for their dogs, people will ride on them, and they will bring dogs with very long ears.'"

Kalaniopuu saw that the discussion was getting nowhere and brought it to an end.

"My runners say that these mysterious marvels are moving down along the coast," he announced. "They should be opposite our camp tomorrow. Then we will go out to greet them and learn the answers to all our questions."

The next morning, which was Monday, November 30, 1778, the entire court was up with the sun. And there, sure enough, slowly rounding the headland to the north, were the two floating islands.

"E-ha!" exulted the stout priest. "It is just as I said! They are *heiaus*, temples of the god Lono. See the ladders going up to his altars in the clear skies."

"No," said Kamehameha. "It is just as I thought. They are great canoes with sails. More huge than we have thought possible, but still canoes. And the people in them are men like ourselves."

As for Kalaniopuu, he donned his feather cape and helmet and motioned for his courtiers to embark with him in the royal double canoe. They glided swiftly out toward the nearer of the high wooden walls.

Figures could be seen standing at the top of the wall behind a railing, figures that were strangely dressed, but smiling and waving in a friendly manner. A rope ladder hung down the wall. The king seized it and mounted unsteadily to the crowded platform.

There a tall, lean man with keen eyes and a tight but genial smile stepped forward, and Kalaniopuu shook hands with Captain James Cook of the British Navy.

The "floating islands" were two English ships with the very appropriate names of *Resolution* and *Discovery*. Two and a half years before, Captain Cook had sailed out of Plymouth on the last of three voyages that were to make him the world's foremost explorer and navigator. On the first two he had drawn the world a picture of its southern hemisphere and had thrown open to colonizers the vast lands of Australia and New Zealand.

The purpose of this third voyage was to answer a question that had intrigued sailors since the days of Magellan. Was there really a Northwest Passage, an easy route north of Canada from Europe to the rich Indies?

In 1776 Captain Cook was sent out to attack the problem from the Pacific end. On his way north, on January 8, 1778, he discovered two uncharted islands, Kauai and Niihau of the Hawaiian group. He named them the Sandwich Islands for the first lord of the Admiralty, the Earl of Sandwich, one of whose ancestors had given his name to a piece of meat between two slices of bread.

Captain Cook spent two weeks at Kauai and then went off to examine the coasts of Canada and Alaska. Now, ten months later, he was back to have a closer look at his discovery and to give his men a rest before another try at the Northwest Passage. The explorer thought it a piece of luck that communication with these islanders would present no problem. They spoke a language very much like that of Tahiti, with which most of the Englishmen on the ships were familiar. As soon as the first words of greeting had been spoken, Kalaniopuu gave this foreign chief who called himself "Kapene Kuka" a friendship offering of half a dozen small pigs. Then he introduced his son, his nephew Kamehameha, and the other people of his retinue.

For over an hour the Hawaiians were conducted open-mouthed about the ship, exclaiming at the many wonderful things they saw. What excited their interest most of all was the metal of which the ship's implements and fittings were made. Save for a few bits of iron that had floated in from the outside world on driftwood, there was no metal on the islands.

The king declined an invitation to spend the night aboard the *Resolution,* but asked that his son and Kamehameha might stay instead. While the ships cruised slowly southward, Kamehameha ate dinner in the cabin. He learned much about "Beretanee," the far-off country from which these ships had come. And more important, he convinced himself that these foreigners came as friends, that they had not come to seize the land. Next morning he and his companions bade their hosts farewell and sailed back to Maui in their canoe that had been towed astern all night.

For six weeks the English ships cruised leisurely around the islands of Hawaii, surveying the coast and trading with the natives. Cook and his men had never before met so friendly and trusting a people. Often the chiefs would send out canoeloads of food and not come aboard until later to be paid. But they were good businessmen. Once having set a price, they would carry their goods back to the beach rather than accept less.

On January 16, 1779, the ships had rounded the southern tip of Hawaii and were standing off the entrance of Kealakekua Bay. To examine the anchorage Captain Cook sent his cartographer, William Bligh, the same Bligh who ten years later was to become famous when mutineers ran off with his ship, the *Bounty*.

Two large villages stood on the shore about a mile and a half apart, reported Mr. Bligh. The one on the north arm of the bay, Kaawaloa, was the seat of the royal court. The other one, Kekua, was built around the massive *heiau* of Lono. Along the shore between the towns stretched a vertical cliff nearly a thousand feet high and pitted with the burial caves of chiefs.

Although most of the shoreline was strewn with boulders, there was a strip of clear sand near the temple and also a good well of fresh water. Cook was satisfied and brought the ships to anchor between the two towns and about seven hundred yards off the face of the cliff.

A vast crowd of islanders had gathered to see the floating *heiaus* of Lono, or perhaps even to catch a glimpse of the god himself. For the local priests, either believing it themselves or thinking it a good chance to build up prestige, had told the people that this was indeed the return of Lono to his home town of Kealakekua.

Thousands lined the shore and hundreds more, in canoes, on surfboards, or just swimming like golden-brown fish, surrounded the ships. And the awesome presence of a god did not at all hinder them from swarming up the sides and mingling with the sailors in a scene of laughing, noisy confusion.

In the midst of the hubbub, a tall young chief boarded the *Resolution* and sought out Captain Cook. He introduced himself as Palea, an officer in the service of King Kalaniopuu. The king and his army had not yet returned from Maui, he said, but were expected soon. In the meantime, was there any way he could be of assistance?

"Yes," replied Cook. "I would be obliged if you could do something about these throngs of people on the ships. They make it quite impossible for the seamen to do their work."

The authority of the warrior was evidently very great. He strode into the mob, pushing and shouting commands, and in no time at all the decks were cleared.

Captain Cook summed up the feelings of his crews at this time in the last words he wrote in the official journal of the voyage:

Perhaps there were few on board who now lamented our having failed in our endeavours to find a Northern passage homeward last summer. To this disappointment we owed our having it in our power to visit the Sandwich Islands, and to enrich our voyage with a discovery which though the last, seemed, in many respects, to be the most important that had hitherto been made by Europeans, throughout the extent of the Pacific Ocean.

CHAPTER 4

Pigs for the Lono

A WEEK PASSED before Kalaniopuu and Kamehameha returned with the army from Maui. In the meantime the Englishmen were well taken care of by the leading citizens of Kealakekua.

Captain Cook had just gone to the cabin after seeing his ships safely anchored when Palea appeared at the door with a little shriveled old man. He had the air of being some sort of dignitary, but his appearance was anything but impressive. His eyes were watery and red-rimmed, and his body was patched with a white scale, the result of drinking too much awa. Palea introduced him as Koa, one of the local priests.

Koa unfolded a piece of red tapa cloth and solemnly draped it about Captain Cook's shoulders. Then he took a small pig from an attendant. Chanting a religious formula, he presented the animal to the captain. To Cook there was nothing remarkable about this. He had received the same homage the year before at Kauai, and at the Friendly Islands and others he had visited. It appeared to be a Polynesian gesture of honor to a notable visitor, like firing a salute from the ships' guns.

Koa said the real purpose of his call was to conduct Captain Cook ashore. The presentation of the pig was a mere preliminary. Now he must be welcomed at a full-dress ceremony at the *heiau*. Cook decided to humor the *kahuna* and motioned to Lieutenant King and Mr. Bayly, the astronomer of the expedition, to go along.

Koa directed the rowers to Kekua, the village at the south end of the cliff. When the party pushed off from the *Resolution* the beach was crowded with people, but, as soon as it was clear that Cook was coming ashore, they melted away. By the time the boat came to a stop on the strip of sand, only a handful of Hawaiians, lying prostrate on their faces, were in sight.

Four priests carrying wands tipped with tufts of dog hair met the boat and led the way to the temple. As they walked they called out what sounded like the announcement of heralds. The only word the Englishmen could make out was "Lono."

The *heiau* was a great stone platform overlooking the sea. It was forty yards long, Lieutenant King estimated, and about half as broad, with a wooden fence around the edge. The posts were topped with blanched skulls, relics of the human sacrifices that were customary at the death of a chief. A ramp led to the top. There stood two grotesque wooden idols to which Captain Cook was solemnly presented.

With a priest on each hand, the navigator was guided across the hot stone pavement to the far side of the *heiau*. Lieutenant

King and Mr. Bayly tagged along with Palea. No one paid any attention to them, and they were free to gaze about like a pair of tourists. They saw that their commander was being taken to a large altar.

Twelve wooden images of gods were arranged in a rough semicircle. In front of the central one, which was draped with red tapa cloth because it was Kalaniopuu's personal god, stood a table. Offerings of bananas, coconuts, and pieces of sugar cane lay piled underneath it. On the table sprawled the decaying carcass of a pig.

"Those things were not put there this morning I'll wager," whispered Mr. Bayly to Lieutenant King. "Did you ever smell such a stench?"

"It's enough to knock one over even back here," answered King. "I don't see how the captain stands it up where he is with that pig right under his nose."

Koa had led Captain Cook up to the table and had lifted the pig. The animal was so rotten that his fingers sank into the flesh. Holding it out toward Cook in the usual ceremonial manner, the old priest was going through another lengthy prayer. The captain endured it all resignedly, holding his breath until he was red in the face. He would go through with this if it killed him. Koa finished at last and let the pig drop to the pavement with a squashy thud.

The next part of the ceremony took place on a high, rickety platform supported by five poles. As Koa and Captain Cook climbed to the top, the flimsy structure swayed and creaked until the two watchers expected to see it collapse any minute.

"Regular game of follow-my-leader the captain is playing," remarked Lieutenant King.

"Yes," Bayly answered. "And here comes another pig. Every time he turns around somebody pushes a pig at him."

"Well," said King, "at least this time it's a fresh one."

Ten priests bearing a trussed live pig and a large piece of red tapa cloth had just entered the *heiau*. They advanced to the scaffolding and handed up their burdens. Koa draped the tapa over Cook's shoulders and repeated the ritual of a few minutes before. While he held the pig out toward the captain, he chanted an ancient hymn, accompanied by the other priests:

> O Lono, of the various bodies in the heavens—
> The long cloud,
> The small cloud,
> The billowing and the spread-out cloud—
> Accept these offerings,
> Living things from the chief to the family on
> the shining cloud and in the floating land.

As the chant ended, Koa lifted the squealing pig high above his head and dashed it to death on the stone floor of the temple. To Captain Cook's great relief, Koa now indicated that he might climb down from the tottering platform.

Koa led the way along the semicircle of images. Before each one he snapped his fingers contemptuously and said something in a sneering tone to show that he thought them of small account compared to the god of Kalaniopuu. When he came to that one he kissed it reverently and prostrated himself before it, motioning his guest to do likewise. Well, thought Cook, this is certainly a strange god to worship. But he did as the priest wished.

The rites in honor of Captain Cook were concluded with a *luau*, or dinner. Koa took the guests to a part of the *heiau* that was about three feet lower than the rest, a sort of sunken open-air banquet hall. Cook was given the place of honor between two large idols.

A party of priests brought in the food: sweet potatoes, breadfruit, coconuts, a huge bowl of poi, and, of course, a roast pig. Sitting down opposite their guests, the priests began serving the meal. Some broke open the coconuts and cut up the pig. Others prepared the awa, busily chewing up the bitter roots and straining the juice through a piece of tapa cloth into a bowl.

While the food was being made ready, one of the priests chewed a lump of coconut meat to an oily pulp. Wrapping it in tapa, he rubbed it over the captain's head and face and hands. Lieutenant King could feel Cook's hand tighten on his arm. Gad, King thought, I hope there isn't much more of this sort of thing. The old boy is about ready to blow up.

There was more—and worse. The bowl of awa was handed round for everyone to taste. Then the Englishmen found out that Hawaiian courtesy included the actual feeding of guests.

The chief Palea broke off a choice morsel of pork and held it to Lieutenant King's mouth, saying, "Eat, Tini!" King did not mind this, as Palea was scrupulously clean. He thought it an amusing experience. But with Captain Cook it was a different story. He was to be fed by Koa. When he saw the unsavory old man's skinny fingers dangling a piece of meat in front of his face, the same fingers that only a few minutes before had handled the stinking mass of putrid hog, it nearly turned his stomach. He controlled his feelings enough merely to shake his head.

Koa was puzzled. The meat smelled delicious. And then, as if to show Cook how good it was, the *kahuna* popped the morsel into his own mouth, chewed it a second or two, and offered it again. Pretending not to see it, Cook stood up and said he must get back to his ship. He presented the priests with some nails from his pocket and was led back to the beach by the four heralds with the dog-hair wands.

The priests of the *heiau* remained friends of the English from first to last, and honored Captain Cook with the title of "Lono." Whenever he went ashore, one of them met him to serve as herald, shouting to the islanders to prostrate themselves. This same herald—"the tabu man," the sailors called him—would even accompany Cook back to the *Resolution* to see that the people in canoes left off paddling and lay down in their boats until "the Lono" had passed.

The morning after their arrival found the crews of both ships hard at work. There were a thousand and one jobs to be done. Months of cruising in the rough northern seas had been hard on all the gear. The hulls were in need of calking and painting, and the sails and rigging were badly worn. The astronomer's instruments had to be set up on shore so that he could make accurate observations. Flour, gunpowder, and such perishable stores must be broken out and examined, and innumerable hogs must be salted down and packed into casks. Lieutenant King was put in charge of the parties of sailmakers and carpenters who were to live on the beach. He was ordered to set up an observatory for Mr. Bayly, so located that it might also serve as a guard post for the working parties.

Having enlisted the help of Palea, he went ashore with Corporal of Marines John Ledyard, a young American adventurer from Groton, Connecticut, who had signed up for the voyage. Palea showed "Tini" various open spaces in the village. When King objected to one of them because it was too small, the helpful chief immediately offered to have some of the surrounding houses pulled down. Fortunately for their occupants, however, King decided on an unused field near the *heiau* that had the advantage of lying near the shore and being enclosed by a stone wall.

Lieutenant King's biggest worry when he was given this shore assignment had been how he would keep the islanders from interfering with the work. Out on the ships, hundreds of men and women began swarming aboard as soon as it was daylight and stood watching the most ordinary operations like curious children. Every hour or so Palea had to drive them off so that the sailors could get on with their tasks. Then the whole crowd would dive laughing into the sea, and ten minutes later all would be back on board again.

But at the observatory Palea removed the difficulty very effectively. He went to the near-by *heiau* and returned with a priest carrying some sticks with bits of white tapa cloth tied to them. When they saw him approaching, the villagers who had already gathered ran off the field and jumped over the wall. They knew what was coming. The *kahuna* walked sedately around the field setting up his sticks at the corners. The area was now tabu. Men might enter the enclosure only with Lieutenant King's permission. Women could not set foot in it in any circumstances.

This arrangement certainly speeded up the work, but it did not at all please the marines. They had pictured this shore duty as a sort of soldier's delight—nothing to do but talk and joke with crowds of laughing *wahines*. Now the girls could come no nearer than the stone wall. The priest had considerately left it outside the limits of the tabu, and from daylight to dark it served as a grandstand for the curious and fascinated villagers.

CHAPTER 5

"I Give You My Name"

AT THE HEAD of a fleet of over one hundred war canoes, Kamehameha and the king swept into Kealakekua Bay from the north.

During the voyage from Maui, Kamehameha had convinced his uncle that the visitors were mortal men, not gods. And so instead of hurrying to greet Captain Cook, the king passed the two anchored ships and went straight to the *heiau* with his chiefs to give thanks to the gods for his safe return.

The next morning Kalaniopuu extended a formal welcome to Captain Cook. Three big double canoes carried the royal party out to the ships. The leading canoe, with its tall lobster-claw sail, was the king's. On the central platform stood Kalaniopuu with Kamehameha and the other high chiefs of his court, splendid in their glossy feather cloaks and helmets.

In the second canoe rode the high priest Kau with the sacred idols laid out on a carpet of red tapa cloth. The grotesque faces, with their oyster shell eyes and distorted mouths set with dogs' teeth, grinned up at the blue sky. The third boat was piled high with hogs and vegetables.

The king's progress was very impressive, for the bay was silent save for the continuous deep-voiced chanting of the priests. The stately procession swung out past the *Resolution* and moved on to the *Discovery*. Then, instead of heading back to the flagship as the officers expected, it continued on toward the strip of beach near the observatory. Captain Cook saw that evidently the reception was to be held on dry land. Jumping into a boat with Captain Clerke of the *Discovery* and some other officers, he was pulled swiftly ashore and arrived at almost the same time as the king.

Lieutenant King, in the meantime, had drawn up his marines to receive the visitors and conduct them to the large observatory tent. Cook and his party entered the tent just after the Hawaiians had sat down. Kalaniopuu rose and advanced to greet them. The aged king took off his own yellow feather cloak and draped it about the captain's shoulders and placed a feather helmet on his head.

"I give you my name," he said, "and I take yours. You are Kalaniopuu. I am Kapene Kuka."

This was the formal exchange of names. Through all the islands of the Pacific there was no stronger pledge of esteem and friendship. The captain could not help feeling a bit self-conscious in his strange costume, but he was quite overcome by the honor that it symbolized.

During this ceremony Captain Cook found his eyes being

drawn again and again to the sternly set face of Kamehameha. Was the warrior chief scowling, or was this his customary grim expression? At any rate, thought Cook, his is the fiercest countenance I have ever seen in my life.

Half an hour later the officers witnessed an incident that caused them to regard Kamehameha as something of a tyrant. Captain Cook invited Kalaniopuu and the chiefs to return with him to the *Resolution*. When they arrived on board, Palea, who had remained on the ship, was standing among the waiting officers. Kamehameha evidently looked on this as an affront to the king. With an angry gesture he stepped up to the young chief.

"Get off this ship!" he ordered.

Now during the past week Palea and Lieutenant King had become the best of friends. They had exchanged names, in fact. King had his mouth open to protest, but he thought it better not to interfere, and so did Captain Cook. Palea, who was a chief of no small consequence himself, went over the side instantly. It was striking evidence of the personal power of Kamehameha at court.

Captain Cook cleared the atmosphere by inviting the Hawaiians into the cabin for refreshments. He gave Kalaniopuu a fine linen shirt and buckled his own sword around the old monarch's waist. It was perhaps a poor return for the gorgeous cloak and helmet, he felt, but he could see that the king was pleased.

The day after the formal reception Kamehameha visited the *Resolution* with a fine present of hogs and fruit. Captain Cook noticed that no matter what they talked of, one topic was sure to come up over and over—the sword he had given to the king. The captain had an idea. He asked to see the chief's *pahua*, the polished hardwood dagger that hung at his waist.

"May I keep this until tomorrow?" asked Cook. "I would like to have a drawing of it made."

When Kamehameha returned the next morning, he was handed his *pahua*.

"E-ha!" he exclaimed.

It was not the wooden one; it was iron. The ship's armorer had fashioned it exactly like the original. Kamehameha could not have been more pleased if its hilt had been studded with precious stones.

"You keep the wooden one for a remembrance," he said to Cook. "It is of no use to me now."

Kamehameha never hesitated to adopt any new thing that he saw was superior to the old. He spent several hours watching the armorers working at their forge. Then he went ashore and set some of his own men to try heating pieces of rough iron and beating them into shape with stones.

It did not take the Hawaiians long to realize how much better than wood this hard material was for tools and weapons. They became so avid for metal that they would sell three or four small pigs for a medium-sized nail. And not all of them could resist the temptation to help themselves if they got the chance. The sailors had to keep a close watch on the ships' belaying pins and other iron objects.

One morning half a dozen ingenious divers were found hard

at work under water prying out the nails that fastened the *Discovery's* copper sheathing. The helpful Palea was consulted. He plummeted into the bay and in a few seconds emerged, dragging up one of the offenders by the hair.

"Shall I kill him?" Palea shouted from the water.

Captain Clerke was content to have the culprit triced up to the rigging and given a taste of a rope's end. There were no more attempts on the sheathing.

The days passed pleasantly for Hawaiians and Englishmen alike. Every day parties of officers made short sight-seeing tours into the surrounding country. They were greeted everywhere with kindness and hospitality. Housewives offered them coconut milk and other refreshments. Chattering groups of boys and girls skipped along beside them, urging the foreigners at every open glade to stop awhile and be entertained with singing and dancing.

One adventurous party, including midshipman George Vancouver and the American marine corporal Ledyard, attempted the ambitious project of climbing to the summit of Mauna Loa. The great size of the volcano—it is nearly fourteen thousand feet high—had deceived them into imagining it to be quite close, a two days' trip at the most. Actually they were away for six days and returned without having come anywhere near their goal. But they had a thrilling tour of the Hawaiian countryside.

Their guides led them first through a belt of well-tended fields planted with taro and sweet potatoes. These plantations were separated by what the explorers thought the most beautiful fences imaginable, loose stone walls with rows of green sugar cane planted along each side. They made their way through forests of koa and sandalwood trees along paths used by the men who collected red and yellow feathers for the chiefs' cloaks and helmets. Occasionally they came across half-finished canoes, huge logs that were being hollowed out before being dragged to the seashore miles away.

Deep in the forest they found the hut of a hermit. Years ago, the guides said, he had been a great chief and warrior, but he had long since retired from the villages. The old man himself waved cheerfully to them from his door. The presence of these strange people did not seem to surprise him in the least.

While the ships were in the bay an old sailor named William Watman died of a stroke. He was the first white man to be buried in the islands, and his funeral was a curious blend of pagan and Christian ritual. At Kalaniopuu's request the grave was dug within the sacred precincts of the *heiau*. The local priests attended and listened reverently while Captain Cook read the Anglican burial service. Just before the sailors began to shovel in the earth, the priests laid on the rude coffin an offering of fruit and a small pig, and for three nights afterward they gathered at the grave to chant Hawaiian prayers for the dead.

One day Kamehameha asked Captain Cook to permit the sailors to attend an exhibition of *mokomoko*, Hawaiian-style boxing. They found it quite different from the boxing matches they were used to. Around a long, level space a boisterous crowd was gathered. When the judges gave the signal, two contestants stepped into the ring.

At first the sailors were puzzled and amused.

"Did they say this was to be a boxing match?" asked one, laughing.

"Looks more like a dance to me," said another.

The boxers were slowly strutting around each other exchanging contemptuous glances and gestures. As they walked they lifted their feet high behind them and drew their hands along the soles. But this preliminary grandstand play was soon over. The boxers began aiming powerful straight-arm swings at each other's heads. These were dodged or parried for a time. Then one of the men caught his opponent off balance and floored him with a crashing blow to the side of his head.

The match was a continuous affair. As soon as one man was knocked down, another immediately stepped up to fight the victor.

The last islander on his feet challenged any one of the sailors to a bout. There were no takers. This South Seas style of boxing might look unscientific, but none of the sailors wanted to be on the receiving end of one of those mighty buffets.

At the end of January Captain Cook informed the king that he planned to leave Hawaii in a few days. Kalaniopuu sent runners to all the surrounding villages ordering the people to bring in their hogs and vegetables as a farewell present.

Kamehameha heard Cook's announcement with a sigh of relief. He knew that his uncle's people were not finding it easy to feed their guests for so long a time and he was afraid some unfriendliness might develop. The chiefs got paid for the food that had been going to the ships, but in the feudal organization of Hawaiian society it was the working people who supplied it.

"Good," the people now said to one another. "Those great canoes swallow up food as did the sea monsters in the old tales."

"Yes. If they stayed here much longer there would be no more to eat in Hawaii than there is in their own country."

"A-we! Their famine must have been very bad. But they have plenty of pigs and sweet potatoes to take back."

One thing that puzzled the average Hawaiian was the reason these foreign men had come to the islands. It soon became clear that they had not come to fight. But why else would men cross the seas in such large canoes?

The most popular explanation was a famine in that far-off "Beretanee," as the wanderers called their home. Hadn't everyone noticed how thin and hungry they were when they arrived, and how ravenously they ate? And all the food that had been loaded into the ships. No doubt they were taking that back to their hungry women and children. The Hawaiians could never understand why the sailors had not brought along their families.

Some of the islanders did not hesitate to let their visitors know that feeding them was becoming burdensome. Lieutenant King saw a group of them good-naturedly pinching the arms and patting the bellies of the sailors.

"E-ha! You're certainly getting fine and fat now," they said. "Why not go home and come back next breadfruit season? Then there will be plenty of food again."

Two days before sailing time, the ships' cooks announced that they were out of wood for the galley stoves. Cut wood was scarce at Kealakekua, and time was short. Captain Cook asked Lieutenant King to see if he could buy the heavy rail fence that surrounded the *heiau*. The lieutenant was shocked at the idea. How could he possibly approach the friendly priests with such a suggestion?

Orders were orders, however, so he sought out the head priest, Kau, and reluctantly explained his mission. He expected the *kahuna* to cry out in horror at so sacrilegious a proposal. Instead, Kau gave his immediate consent.

"Take it all for your ships, Tini," he said, "and say nothing of paying me. I give it to you. My people will soon build another fence. I will tell them to help your men carry it to the shore."

A little later King noticed a sailor and a native carrying off a large wooden image. It was, indeed, the last one of the semicircle before which Captain Cook had been honored two weeks earlier.

Again he went to Kau, and found him talking with Kamehameha.

"It is all right," Kamehameha said. "They are not the gods. They are only wooden symbols of the gods that we ourselves have made. Every *heiau* has others like them. We will make more. But," he added firmly, "I would like your men to bring back the image of Kalaniopuu's god. It is a very old one."

After promising to return the image, King was about to turn away when Kamehameha took him by the arm.

"Come into this house with me, Tini," he said. "We want to talk with you."

Seated in the hut was Kalaniopuu himself. The king greeted the officer warmly, and even his stern-faced nephew wore a genial smile. Kalaniopuu opened the business.

"Tini," he said, "I will not waste words. My nephew Kamehameha thinks it would be a good thing for Hawaii if one of the men of Beretanee would live with us and help us, and I agree with him. We like you best. We want you to stay."

Young Lieutenant King looked from one to the other. What could he say? How could he refuse such a flattering offer without hurting their feelings? He told them he would have to ask Captain Cook. And later Kamehameha and his uncle were satisfied when Cook said he would give his answer next winter when he planned to return to the islands.

Finally the two ships were ready to sail and stood slowly out of Kealakekua Bay. The breeze was so light that for two days the squadron made very little progress. Then suddenly the weather changed. The sky became overcast and violent gusts of wind began to blow from the land. It was the beginning of a *kona* storm. With increasing fury the wind and rain lashed the ships until it was blowing a gale. On the fourth morning after they had set sail, it was found that the force of the wind had split the *Resolution's* foremast.

Captain Cook was faced with a problem. Should he return to Kealakekua Bay, or should he run the chance of finding a harbor along the unknown shores of the leeward islands? He thought it better not to take the risk, and ordered his ships to put about and beat their way back against the lessening wind. The decision was to cost him his life.

CHAPTER 6

The Death of a God

WHEN RUNNERS brought the news that the two foreign ships were headed back down the coast toward Kealakekua Bay, a hot dispute began at the royal court. One group of chiefs was against furnishing any more supplies to Captain Cook.

"Our people can bring no more food," they argued. "They have barely enough for themselves. And why is Kapene Kuka coming back so soon? This time he may not come as a friend."

Kamehameha, however, took a different view. He was determined to maintain peace.

"We all wish the foreigners had continued on their way," he said. "But they must have some good reason for changing their plans, and I for one do not think it is unfriendly. The gods of these men favor them with powerful mana. Look at the wonderful things they have that our gods have not granted to us. It will be good to have them as our friends. When they go back to their country, let them tell their king that the people of Hawaii treated them with courtesy and good will."

Kalaniopuu agreed with his nephew and decided that the official policy should be the same friendly one as before. When the ships were at anchor once more in Kealakekua Bay and he learned Captain Cook's reason for returning, the king assured Cook of all possible aid.

It was very evident to the mariners that they were not so welcome this time. No shouting multitude ushered them into the bay. Canoes came out to trade, but the sailors found that prices had gone up sharply. And the Hawaiians again began to steal articles from the ships. One man seized a pair of tongs from the Discovery's forge, leaped over the side into a waiting canoe, and got safely ashore with his prize.

At dawn on Sunday, February 14, 1779, Captain Cook was awakened by Captain Clerke of the *Discovery*, who was in a great state of excitement. During the night someone had stolen the *Discovery's* large cutter from its mooring buoy.

Cook acted immediately. He had decided beforehand just what he would do in a case like this. First he ordered several small boats to maintain a patrol across the entrance of the harbor. No canoes were to be allowed to leave. Then he called his officers together and explained his plan. It was one that he had used successfully to get back stolen articles in other parts of the South Seas. He would go ashore with some marines, persuade the king to come out to the ship, and then hold him hostage until the cutter was restored.

"Sir," inquired one of his officers, "won't the Indians resist an armed landing?"

"I am not worried about that," replied Cook. "They may oppose us, but the first shot from one of our muskets will terrify and disperse them. That is always the case with people who face gunfire for the first time."

While he was talking, the captain carefully loaded his own double-barreled gun, one barrel with a blank charge, the other with a lead ball.

At half past seven in the morning Captain Cook was rowed ashore in a six-oared pinnace filled with marines under the command of a Lieutenant Phillips. The Hawaiians who were on the beach offered no opposition to the landing, but respectfully prostrated themselves as usual before "the Lono."

Cook told them he had come to see Kalaniopuu. One of the men ran off and came back in a few minutes with the king's two young sons. The boys were glad to see Kapene Kuka. He let them visit his ship as often as they pleased and roam all over it. They led their friend to their father's house, a file of marines marching along behind.

The house stood only a hundred yards or so from the beach, and when they reached it Lieutenant Phillips went to the door to announce their visit to the king. The old gentleman was just waking up. When he heard that Kuka was outside, he called his attendants to help make him presentable and stepped out into the sunshine.

"Kuka," he called, "I am glad to see you. You come very early, though. I hope nothing is wrong."

After a brief word of greeting, Captain Cook told the king of the theft of the cutter. Kalaniopuu's face clouded with anger as he listened.

"I am sorry to hear this, Kuka," he said. "I will get the boat back, and whoever stole it shall be turned over to you to be punished."

There could be no doubt of the old man's sincerity. This was certainly the first he knew of the matter. Nevertheless, Cook resolved to go through with his plan, and he invited the king and his sons to spend the day on the *Resolution*. In fact, why not come right now and have breakfast? The boys ran off gleefully to swim out to the pinnace, and the captain and Kalaniopuu began to walk slowly down to the shore. The crowd that had collected made way for them.

Just when it looked as though all would go off smoothly, a shrill voice was heard from the direction of the village calling on Kalaniopuu to stop. Cook turned and saw a stout woman waddling toward them as fast as she could put one fat leg in front of the other. It was one of the king's favorite wives, the mother of the two boys. She came up all out of breath and grasped Kalaniopuu by the arm.

"Don't go! Don't go!" she entreated, with tears streaming down her cheeks.

"What's the matter?" her puzzled husband demanded. "I am only going to the ship with my friend Kapene Kuka."

The queen's voice was pleading and apprehensive. "No, you must stay here. I feel that something bad will happen."

Kalaniopuu turned to Captain Cook with an apologetic shrug. "What foolishness!" he said.

As the king was about to continue toward the beach, Kamehameha stepped from the crowd and faced him. The chief's face was set and determined.

"You shall not go to the ship," he said to his uncle.

When the king hesitated, Kamehameha and another chief each took him by an arm and forced him to sit down on a stone. Kalaniopuu was now too confused to do anything but remain helplessly where they had put him.

Lieutenant Phillips, meanwhile, had been watching the crowd, now numbering about three thousand men and women. If the aged king did not realize Captain Cook's intention, evidently everyone else did. Angry mutterings rose from the mob. Spears and daggers were flourished threateningly. Phillips saw that if it came to a fight his marines would be helpless in that close-packed mass of humanity. He ordered his men to draw up in a line along the water's edge.

Captain Cook knew now that he would never be able to get the king away without bloodshed. He gave up the idea altogether and started toward the beach. In another minute he and the marines would have been safely embarked in the pinnace. But fate had ordered things otherwise.

Up to the shore slid a small dugout. A warrior leaped from it into the shallow water and ran past Cook to the group of chiefs gathered about the king. He shouted his news in a loud voice so that all could hear. The boats patrolling the bay had fired on a canoe and killed a chief, one of the highest-ranking and most popular chiefs of Kalaniopuu's court.

At this announcement all the pent-up excitement of the crowd burst out in an angry roar. The warriors began putting on their thick *lauhala* chest mats and hustling the women and children back to the village. There was a tense moment while each side waited for the other to make a move.

It came from a glowering young warrior, a relative of the slain chief. With a dagger in one hand and a stone in the other, he planted himself in front of Captain Cook and began shouting threats and insults. In a calm, level voice, the captain told him to go away. The man's answer was to draw back his arm to throw the stone.

Cook raised his gun and fired the blank charge. He hoped the noise and flash would cause the crowd to draw back and give his men a chance to reach the boat. Its effect was exactly the opposite. The warrior jumped, but when he found he was uninjured he shouted to his comrades that there was nothing to be afraid of. These banging sticks were harmless!

A chief leaped at Lieutenant Phillips with raised dagger, but the officer caught him under the chin with the butt end of his musket. Stones began to fly. One of them struck a marine on the head and stretched him out on the sand.

There is nothing for it now, decided Cook, but to defend ourselves as best we can.

"Open fire!" he shouted to the marines, and at the same time killed a warrior with the ball from his second barrel.

Cook then gave the order, "Take to the boat!"

The pinnace came in as close as it could, but it was hampered by the shallow water and the showers of stones and the marines standing up to fire.

Kamehameha was horrified when he saw the first quick blows struck. The very thing that he had scoffed at in the council was actually happening. All the weeks of friendly relations with the foreigners would go for nothing. He was just about to step between the two angry groups when the marines fired their volley. That changed everything. Men who killed his warriors were enemies to be attacked and destroyed.

When he saw the marines poking the ramrods into the muzzles of their guns, Kamehameha guessed it was some operation that must be performed before they could fire again. Now was the chance to kill them.

"Attack them now!" he shouted to his men. "Cut them down before they can do more harm!"

Before the marines could finish reloading, the islanders rushed upon them. Four were instantly stabbed to death and the others were forced out into the water. Every last man of them would have been killed if the Hawaiians had not been slowed down by the musket fire from the boat.

Captain Cook was now the only Englishman on the beach. Carrying his gun under his right arm, he stepped into the shallow water and began wading out toward the pinnace. He held his left hand against the back of his head to ward off stones.

For a minute it looked as though he were going to be allowed to reach the boat without being attacked. Then a thin stooping figure brandishing a club scurried into the water behind Cook. It was one of the priests, an old man who had never been friendly toward the foreigners. When he was within reach he struck the captain a heavy blow on the back of the head with his stick and ran back into the crowd.

The blow made Captain Cook stagger and he fell to his knees in the water. He tried to rise, but before he could regain his feet a Hawaiian leaped upon him and stabbed him between the shoulders with an iron dagger. It was one of several that Cook himself had given to the chiefs as presents.

Captain Cook pitched full length into the surf. Yelling warriors crowded about him, holding him under water and stabbing him repeatedly. Before he died he managed to get his head above water and cast a last agonized look toward the men in the pinnace, but they were powerless to aid him.

Aboard the *Resolution*, meanwhile, the ship's guns had been brought to bear on the beach, and now they opened fire. But the Hawaiians had seen the guns being made ready. Many of them merely dispersed, taking the body of Captain Cook with them. Those who remained were safely tucked away in a ditch or behind a stone wall by the time the first shot came over. The brief bombardment caused little damage—one or two huts were knocked over—but it made a deep impression on the mind of Kamehameha.

The young chief watched the *Resolution*, lying far beyond the reach of any of his weapons, throw great balls of iron into the air. He saw them crash to earth and bound over the grass, knocking down everything in their path. Just so, he had been

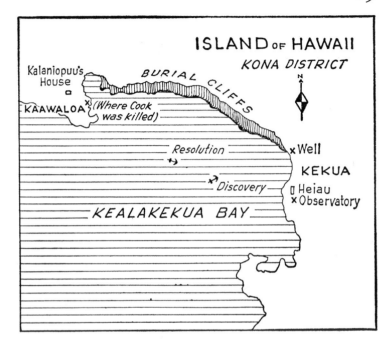

told when he was a boy, did the volcano goddess Pele spew huge rocks from the top of Kilauea.

But those sailors were not gods, he reflected. They were men like himself, only they knew the secret of the volcano. As he watched, the ancient weapons of his people seemed obsolete and worthless. The chief who could command a few of those red-mouthed guns would be master of all the islands.

Kamehameha ran from one place to another to see how the cannonballs behaved after they struck the earth. He wanted to know just how much damage one of them could do before it stopped. In his eagerness he forgot that he himself might be included in the damage.

Suddenly a ball crashed against a rock near where he stood. The warriors who were watching were horrified to see their leader stagger and clap his hand to his head. They rushed out and drew him down behind a wall. Fortunately he had only been stunned by a flying splinter of stone that cut a gash across his cheek.

Although the bombardment ended in a short time, Kamehameha doubted that this was the end of the fighting. The foreigners, he felt sure, would not let the killing of their captain go unavenged. He ordered a large force of warriors to stand ready to meet any hostile move from the ships. Then he conducted his uncle to a place of safety in one of the cliffside caves. There, halfway up the face of the precipice overlooking the bay, the old king was to live until all danger had passed. His cave could be reached only by ropes and even his food had to be lowered to him from above.

Captain Clerke of the *Discovery*, now commander of the expedition, told his officers that he intended to adopt peaceful measures if possible. The islanders had been provoked, he said, and had acted in the heat of passion. They could hardly be blamed for having been afraid of Captain Cook's warlike party, and they had fought only to defend their king. To seek revenge would be cruel and inhuman.

An officer was sent ashore to tell the chiefs there would be no more fighting and to request that the body of Captain Cook be returned to the ships for proper burial. He was told that

Cook's body had been cut up and the pieces distributed among the high chiefs and priests as sacred relics. They would be collected, however, and brought out to the *Resolution*.

One point on which the Englishmen had never been able to satisfy themselves was whether or not the Hawaiians were cannibals. The officer decided to settle the question now.

"Did your people eat any of the body?" he asked.

The chiefs stared in astonishment.

"Is that what is done in your country?" one of them asked.

True to their promise, the Hawaiians delivered the remains of the great navigator carefully wrapped in white tapa cloth. His bones were nailed in a coffin and buried from the *Resolution* in the waters of Kealakekua Bay.

Before the ships set sail that same evening they were surrounded by canoes. Many of the chiefs paddled out to say "Aloha" and express their grief over the unhappy doings of the past few days.

One question the people asked themselves over and over: "When will the Lono return, and what will he do to us then?" For whatever Kamehameha and some of the more sophisticated chiefs might believe, there was not the slightest doubt in the minds of the majority of Hawaiians that in the person of "Kapene Kuka" they had looked on the immortal god Lono.

From a lofty lookout post on the top of Kealakekua cliff Kamehameha watched the *Resolution* and the *Discovery* glide through the moon-silvered water. His eyes followed the ships, but his thoughts were in the future.

Until the exciting reports had come from Kauai a year ago,

he had never given a thought to the possibility that other men might live beyond the rim of the island seas. And then these enterprising foreigners, godlike in their cleverness and knowledge, had burst in like visitors from another world. Now they were leaving, and not as enemies he hoped.

Kapene Kuka had once said that even if he did not return certainly other men from his country of Beretanee, and from other great countries, would come to Hawaii. Kamehameha could see them now, sailing majestically into Kealakekua Bay in their incredible canoes, bringing guns and wonderful tools and other undreamed-of things.

Kamehameha's plans soared at the thought of it. For with the help of such men, what would not be possible for him!

CHAPTER 7

The War God Must Be Served

THE STRAIN of the last Maui campaign and the excitement of having his island discovered had made Kalaniopuu realize that he was getting old. He was tired; and he was disappointed, too. Years and years of fighting and nothing to show for it but some sort of indefinite promise that his son should have Maui after Kahekili's death. And now there was a rebellious chief in the Puna district who had to be taken care of. Why not let younger and stronger men do the heavy work, and spend one's last days in ease and comfort?

So about a year after the departure of the English ships Kalaniopuu summoned his chiefs to a council. Over the mountain trails they came with their families and servants. They were eager and excited, for the rumor had gone out that the king was going to name his successor. At the meeting place they gathered under the trees to speculate on who it would be.

In one group the discussion was especially warm and loud.

Keawe the Wanderer, chief of the Hilo district, was shouting to make himself heard.

"What is there to discuss?" he asked. "There should be no doubt at all. Only one man can follow the king, his son Kiwalao. His mother is the sacred chieftess Kalola, and his blood is the most noble in the kingdom."

"That may be," cried the warrior Kekuhaupio. "But I say Kamehameha is twice the man. Never have we seen such a fighter, young as he is, even if I say so who taught him."

"True enough," said another. "But do we want to spend the rest of our lives fighting? Kamehameha would never be happy unless he had us at war with someone or other."

Kekuhaupio was disgusted. "What woman's talk! You would rather hoe your taro patch, I suppose, and let Kahekili swoop down from Maui and make a slave of you."

The arrival of Kalaniopuu put a stop to the quarrel. Dignified and regal in his state robe of yellow mamo feathers, the old king faced the semicircle of chiefs.

"Our taxgatherers have just returned from Puna saying that the chief Imakakaloa refuses to pay his tribute and is in open revolt against us. I am an old man now and it will not be long before the black cloth covers me. I think it is good, before our warriors march to Puna, that I should say who is to rule after me."

The king fixed a steady gaze on the chiefs, as though defying any one of them to find fault with his choice.

"Kiwalao, my son, shall be king. When I am gone, serve him and obey him."

This announcement set off a general hubbub. There were cheers, of course, for the future king. But there were murmurs of disappointment also, loud and numerous enough to be heard. Kamehameha's face was set and inscrutable. Kalaniopuu did not move and obviously had something more to say. The crowd became quiet and the king spoke again.

"Our enemies are many and we must fight to live. We must never fail to honor him who sends our spears straight and turns aside those of our enemies, the sacred war god, Kukailimoku."

At mention of the dread name a murmur of awe and reverence arose from the people. Many glanced toward the *heiau* where the idol rested—the ferocious head of yellow feathers with its staring mother-of-pearl eyes and its grinning mouth set with sharks' teeth.

"His *heiau* must be cared for and his worship never neglected," the king went on. "There is one among us who is suited best of all for this high trust, for his achievements show him to be beloved of the god. When I die the custody of the war god shall pass to my nephew, Kamehameha."

The young prince's heart leaped within his breast. Let Kiwalao be named king now. Was not the war god Ku the maker of kings?

An expedition under Kamehameha and Kiwalao set out for Puna to put down the rebellious Imakakaloa. The campaign was a long one, for the rebel knew every ambuscade and hiding place in his territory. But Kamehameha's pursuit was relentless, and the chief was eventually cornered and killed. His body was carried to a near-by temple to be sacrificed to Kukailimoku.

Kiwalao, representing his father, was to make the sacrifice. He was a mild-mannered, rather shy young man, and the crowd of silent priests and warriors made him decidedly uncomfortable. He was very conscious, too, of his stern-faced cousin standing with folded arms in the front rank of the nobles.

Kiwalao could feel his knees shake as he advanced toward the stiff corpse. He reached to lift the body, but the open, staring eyes unnerved him. He decided to make a preliminary offering of a pig.

As Kamehameha watched his cousin take up the carcass of the pig, disgust showed plainly in his face and then gave way to a look of determination. What nonsense was this? The *kahunas* had made enough preliminary offerings. And was not he the one who was to be custodian of the war god?

Kamehameha stepped forward, lifted the body of the rebel chief in his arms, and walked toward the altar. There was a gasp from the crowd, and then dead silence. Kiwalao, still holding the pig, was forced to stand aside. He trembled with shame and anger.

Kamehameha began to chant in a strong, clear voice and completed the ritual. Then he turned and faced the other worshipers, tall and proud before the altar of his war god and caring for no man's opinion. For several seconds no one moved. Then Kiwalao, confused and silent, turned and walked out of the *heiau*.

News of what had happened in the temple spread swiftly through the villages and caused a sensation. People stopped their work to gather and gabble. The king's own son, who was to be the next king, had been publicly thrust aside and insulted! And in the sacred confines of the *heiau!* Kamehameha would pay dearly for his hotheadedness, no doubt. A shame, too, for he was a great athlete and warrior. He was the sort of leader a man would be glad to follow, in spite of his stern manner. E-ha! Even now he was probably lying dead.

The priests and nobles gathered about Kalaniopuu. It began to look as though Kamehameha had unwisely played into the hands of those who feared him and hoped for his destruction. Several of the chiefs had plans of their own for arranging matters after the old king's death, and there was no place in their schemes for anyone as ambitious as Kamehameha.

"Your son will not rule the land after you, O king," prophesied an old *kahuna.* "As his cousin pushed him aside from the altar, so will he push him from the throne."

The wily Keawe of Hilo spoke up. "It was foretold at his birth that this man would be a rebel, a maker of trouble for the chiefs. Let him be put to death now for this insult so that we may serve your son in peace."

Kalaniopuu was old, but not too slow-thinking to guess why they were so eager to be rid of his nephew. He listened to them in silence and managed to dismiss them without committing himself.

He waited until most of the people were in their homes preparing the evening meal. Then, taking only one attendant, the king went to the eating house of Kamehameha. The young prince had just sat down to some baked fish and a huge bowl of poi. He sprang to his feet when Kalaniopuu entered and then prostrated himself without speaking.

"Rise, my son," said Kalaniopuu gently. "I call you by this name because I love you as a son. Why did you do this rash thing?"

A great weight seemed to lift itself from Kamehameha's heart. His uncle was not angry.

"I beg forgiveness, uncle," he answered. "I did not mean any insult to you or to your son. I do not know why I acted so. As I watched the ceremony, suddenly it seemed as though only I were there in the temple. Something said to me, 'You must complete this sacrifice!' I stepped forward and . . . well, that is how it was. I had no——"

Kalaniopuu interrupted him in a low, urgent tone.

"The will of the gods is not known to us until they think proper to reveal it. You are a born king. After my death, what is to be, will be. But now, my son, you are in danger. There are many who envy you and fear you, and they are crying out for your life. I am too old and weak to stand against them.

"Take the war god and go at once to your estates in Kohala. There among your faithful warriors you will be safe until this affair is forgotten. Go now, this very night. It is my command to you, and may the gods keep you."

The old king embraced his nephew whom, as events were to show, he never saw again. Tears were in his eyes as he turned and left the house.

So once more Kamehameha went into seclusion in order to save his life. He lost no time in obeying his uncle's command. No good could come from his remaining at the court. He would use this retirement to improve his estates.

A year or so later, in the spring of 1782, old, worn-out Kalaniopuu died. His death was the signal for the intrigues that had been smoldering among the chiefs to burst into flame. Kiwalao, the new king, would have the privilege of redistributing the land among the nobles if he wished. And his uncle, the crafty Keawe of Hilo, was greedy for the rich province of Kona.

Most of that district was held by Keeaumoku, who had always been a stanch supporter of the dead king, and by other chiefs friendly to Kamehameha. Keawe had the new king completely under his influence, and Kamehameha had not been seen at court for a year. What was to be done?

The answer came from Kekuhaupio, who years ago had taught Kamehameha the art of warfare.

"Let me go to Kohala and talk with Kamehameha," he suggested. "Let me tell him how things stand. He will not have forgotten his friends, and he has no liking for Kiwalao. He is the greatest warrior in Hawaii and a hero to the people. I will bring him back to be our leader."

Kekuhaupio found Kamehameha at work with his people laying out a new taro field. For a year now he had ignored politics and the affairs at court. He had been busy cultivating his lands, building new fish ponds along the shore, and widening trails through the forests. But news of Kalaniopuu's death had stirred his ambitions and made him long for action of a different sort.

At sight of his former tutor, Kamehameha gave a cry of joy. Little explaining was necessary between them. While Kekuhaupio was still talking, Kamehameha dropped his digging tool and started toward his house to get ready.

Kamehameha and Kiwalao met at the royal burial place at Honaunau, just south of the bay where Captain Cook had been killed three years before. Outwardly there was no animosity between them. They greeted each other by touching nose to cheek, and mourned together over the remains of Kalaniopuu. But among the nobles the atmosphere was tense with suspicion and mistrust.

That evening the traditional ceremony of awa drinking was held in the king's council house. By the light of burning oily *kukui* nuts, the chiefs of the kingdom seated themselves in a circle. At this ritual the king gave a piece of bitter awa root to each high-ranking chief. The man would chew this to a pulp and then strain the juice through a piece of tapa cloth into a calabash bowl. This juice the king would then drink in recognition of the chief's homage.

Kiwalao distributed the pieces of awa root around the circle, but gave none to Kamehameha.

When he saw this, Kekuhaupio spoke angrily to the new king.

"Give some to your cousin to be chewed," he said.

Kiwalao, who always preferred to avoid open trouble, handed over a piece of the root. All eyes were on them. Would Kamehameha again publicly insult his royal cousin? The prince took the root, chewed it, strained the juice into a calabash, and passed it to the king.

And now it was Kiwalao who did the insulting. Instead of drinking from the bowl, he handed it with a smile to a chief seated next to him. The man raised it to his mouth, but before he could drink, Kekuhaupio sprang up and dashed the bowl from his hand.

"You make a mistake, O king!" the warrior shouted. "The prince Kamehameha does not chew awa for men of that rank. He need chew for no one but the king himself!"

And then the Kona chiefs rose as one man from the circle and with Kamehameha at their head strode from the room.

Next day Kiwalao announced his new distribution of lands. It was just as the Kona chiefs had feared. The greater part of their holdings was stripped from them and given to Kiwalao's scheming uncle, Keawe. Kamehameha's estates, too, were threatened, and there seemed no course for him and his followers but open rebellion.

Actual fighting was started, however, not by Kamehameha, but by the new king's half brother, Keoua of the Scarlet Cloak. He raided a section of Kohala, cutting down valuable coconut trees and killing some of Kamehameha's people.

In the vicious battle that followed, the outcome was decided by the warrior chief Keeaumoku. During the fighting he was wounded and fell to the ground. Seeing this, Kiwalao rushed up to strip him of his battle cape and the chief's amulet that hung about his neck.

"The yellow-backed crab has met his end at last!" Kiwalao exulted.

But he spoke too soon. When he was within easy reach, Keeaumoku raised himself on his elbow and drove his javelin into the king's body. Kiwalao's reign had come to an end. With the king dead, Keawe and Keoua were soon put to flight.

Kamehameha heaped praise on Keeaumoku.

"You are a maker of kings," he said. "In the old days it was you who helped put Kalaniopuu on the throne. And now once more you have made a king."

"You are king indeed," replied Keeaumoku, and all the other chiefs shouted their agreement. "But there are still enemies for my spear to seek out."

CHAPTER 8

The Law of the Splintered Paddle

AND SO BEFORE he had reached his twenty-ninth birthday Kamehameha was king of West Hawaii. He ruled the provinces of Kona, Kohala, and Hamakua. The remainder of the island—Hilo, Puna, and Kau—was divided between Kiwalao's brother, Keoua of the Scarlet Cloak, and his uncle Keawe.

Kamehameha knew that enemies like these did not stay quiet. Before he could have peace, he must eliminate them and make himself master of the whole island. This job proved to be a more difficult task than he anticipated.

It was not that he had an exaggerated opinion of his own ability. True, he did believe that in all Hawaii there was no better leader of men in battle than he, but he was wise enough to realize that there were others who had lived longer and were more experienced. Keeaumoku, for example, and Keku-haupio, and the other Kona chiefs. He formed these veterans into a council which he always consulted before taking any important action.

It was decided to strike first at Hilo, the home territory of Keawe. But that wily old warrior was not to be caught off his guard. He persuaded King Kahekili of Maui to send him reinforcements, and, when Kamehameha's thrust came, he was ready to meet it. It was a simultaneous attack by sea and by land. Keawe threw everything he had against the land army and utterly defeated it. The fleet of war canoes never had a chance to strike. It was all they could do to rescue the land army survivors from the Hilo beaches.

This setback was a staggering shock to Kamehameha. He had imagined that one sharp blow would suffice to crack Keawe. He withdrew to his Hamakua base to lick his wounds and plan the next move. It was then, while all his thoughts were turned to warfare, that Kamehameha learned a valuable lesson in the art of peaceful government.

The people of Hilo had left no doubt as to their feelings toward him, but Kamehameha was not sure that the Puna district was equally hostile. Puna lay just to the south of Hilo, and, if he could establish himself there, his position would be considerably strengthened.

He knew of just the person to tell him what he wished to know. On the Puna coast lived a wise old man who had long been a close friend of the young king. This Kuuhu had once been a chief of importance, but now he lived alone in semi-retirement.

With his usual preference for handling his affairs personally, Kamehameha decided to pay this man a visit. It must be done secretly and at night, for his canoe would have to pass along the hostile coast of Hilo. He ordered his best canoe master to get ready the swiftest outrigger and a crew of expert paddlers, and, as soon as it was dark, he set out on the hazardous trip.

A storm had come up and was lashing the shore, but the skillfully handled canoe made its way steadily through the heavy seas. All night long they paddled. When the sky began to brighten they saw they were near the desired point on the Puna coast. The sea had calmed, and the tired little band headed for the beach.

On the edge of the surf a group of fishermen were preparing their nets and boats for the morning's work. When they saw the strange canoe approaching so swiftly from out of the sunrise, they called to each other in alarm. Shading their eyes, they stood peering intently for a minute. Suddenly one of the men recognized the tall figure standing among the paddlers.

"Run!" he shouted. "Spread the alarm! That is Kamehameha!"

The fishermen began feverishly gathering up their nets to save them from capture, for they represented many hours of tiresome labor.

Kamehameha was grieved to see that his very name spread terror among these Puna people. He must reach them and talk to them. He must convince them he did not come as an enemy. Telling his men to wait for him, he cast aside his cloak and dived into the water. Soon he was only waist deep in the surf. He stood up and began splashing toward the frightened fishermen, shouting to them to stop. They only redoubled their efforts to get away with their nets.

Then one of them, looking back to see how fast their supposed enemy was gaining, gave a cry of joy. They were no longer being pursued!

Under the water, extending out from the edge of the sand, lay a ledge of coral rock full of sharp points and treacherous holes. Kamehameha's foot had become wedged in one of the crevices and he stood helplessly trapped in the surf. Their terrible foe, the unconquerable Kamehameha, was at their mercy! His canoe was far out in the shallow water.

Whooping wildly at their good fortune, the fishermen dropped the nets and ran to their canoes to arm themselves with paddles. Then they waded out to the king and began to beat him over the head. Caught as he was, he could do little to defend himself against the blows that fell from all sides. The paddles made great cuts from which the blood flowed down his face, and he could feel his head beginning to reel.

Fortunately some of the paddles broke under the force of the blows, and his own men were closing in. His warriors did not dare to throw spears from a distance for fear of impaling him. Seeing this new danger, the fishermen abandoned their victim and ran for the trees with the warriors in hot pursuit.

Two men remained to help their badly wounded leader. They chipped the coral to free his foot, and carried him to the house of Kuuhu, which stood near by. The old man drew his friend's cuts together and applied soothing herbs to his bruised body.

Kamehameha had rested and recovered his senses by the time his warriors returned. They had been able to catch only one of the fishermen, and they flung him to his knees before the king. The man was clad only in a malo. With his graying hair he looked to be about fifty years old. He shook with fear, expecting that he had very few more moments to live.

"Look up at me!" commanded Kamehameha, his head still throbbing from the blows. "Are you one of those who struck me with the paddles?"

The man was too terrified to speak. He nodded his head and prostrated himself on the floor of the hut.

"Why did you do it?" asked the king. "I came as a friend."

Something in Kamehameha's tone gave the man courage enough to find his tongue, and now he spoke up boldly.

"We had been told, O king, that you were the enemy of Puna. When we saw you rushing at us we thought you came to plunder us and take our nets and canoes. Those are the most valuable things we have. They take much time to make and we must have them to get our food. A man fights to defend things like that, your Majesty."

As he listened to the man's earnest words, Kamehameha's face became thoughtful. He sat for several minutes in silence before he spoke.

Then he said, "This man is right. What belongs to a man should not be taken from him by force. Everyone should be allowed to do his work in peace. Release him and let him go to his home."

Scarcely able to believe his ears, the fisherman remained

kneeling with bowed head and eyes filled with tears of gratitude.

"Did you break your paddle over my head?" Kamehameha
asked.

Very shamefacedly, the man admitted that he had.

The king turned to one of his followers. "Give him a paddle
from my canoe to replace it," he ordered.

Later, inspired by this incident, Kamehameha proclaimed
one of the great laws of his reign:

"Let the aged, men and women, and little children lie down
and sleep in security along the highway. Let no one molest
them. The penalty is death."

The intention of this edict was to outlaw crimes of violence,
especially against people unable to defend themselves. Kamehameha called the law *Mamalahoe*, "The Law of the Splintered
Paddle," for he was not ashamed to have everyone know how
it had come to be made.

What Kamehameha learned from old Kuuhu about his
chances of occupying Puna is not recorded. Evidently the
advice was not encouraging, for the king called off his campaign to subdue Hilo and led his army back home to Kohala.

The warrior king saw now that the island empire of his
dreams was not to be won by impulsive hit-or-miss methods.
Only by first patiently building up his strength at home could
he hope to make any permanent conquests.

For seven years after the *Resolution* and the *Discovery* sailed
off to the north, no foreign ships stopped at Hawaii. Kameha-

meha often wondered if more would ever come. Or had the killing of Kapene Kuka stamped his people as savage murderers who were not worth visiting?

By this time, however, the account of Captain Cook's third voyage had been published, and the existence of the Sandwich Islands was common knowledge in Europe and America. Ships of all countries sailing the Pacific began to make a point of looking in on this handy stopover. It was one of these ships that carried the first Hawaiian traveler to the outside world.

In 1787 an English merchant skipper named John Meares put in at the island of Kauai and took with him to China one of the local chiefs. His name was Kaiana, and he was a half brother of the kings of Kauai and Maui. When the young warrior, clad in his brilliant feather cape and helmet, stepped ashore at Canton he caused a sensation. Well over six feet tall, he had a handsome, intelligent face and the build of an athlete. His good humor and open-eyed wonder at all the strange things he saw charmed everyone who met him.

After several months at Canton, Kaiana left for home with Captain Douglas, a friend of Meares. On approaching the islands, Douglas learned that the king of Kauai had become jealous of his half brother and was planning to have him killed. Kaiana asked to be taken to Kealakekua Bay, saying that he would enter the service of the king of West Hawaii.

Kamehameha welcomed the young traveler with open arms. He pictured to himself the shocked faces of his rivals to the north when they learned that one of their highest chiefs had come over to the Hawaiian side! And how useful Kaiana would be with his knowledge of foreign ways and his treasure chest full of foreign tools. Five canoes were needed to haul ashore his collection of saws, gimlets, hatchets, knives, carpets, chinaware, and bars of iron. Kamehameha gave his new follower a large tract of land and a place in his council of chiefs, and later made him governor of Puna province.

As later events were to show, this was perhaps the only mistake the king made in his judgment of men. For, unfortunately, behind Kaiana's smiling countenance lay an ambitious and treacherous mind. He had not been long in Hawaii before he began plotting against the very man who had given him a refuge from his enemies. What he hoped to do, it seems, was involve Kamehameha in serious trouble with foreign ships and then, by some means or other, have himself made king in his place.

The scheming fellow saw that he never would be able to induce the king himself to attack a ship. One of Kamehameha's chief desires was to maintain friendly relations with the foreigners who visited his country. He had often made it clear to his chiefs that he wanted no disputes with travelers from beyond the seas.

What Kaiana planned to do was persuade one of the chiefs to seize a ship. He watched and waited, and it was not long until he got his chance. Fortunately, however, the disloyal chief's scheme backfired. Instead of doing Kamehameha an injury, he unintentionally did him a great service.

In the spring of 1790 Kameeiamoku, a hotheaded chief of one of the coastal districts, was struck by a New England trading skipper named Simon Metcalfe. A few days after Metcalfe had left, a small schooner, the *Fair American*, commanded by Metcalfe's son, arrived off Hawaii.

This was Kaiana's opportunity. He persuaded Kameeiamoku to kill the crew and seize the ship. Kamehameha was angry that these chiefs had disobeyed his orders, but he did not punish them. For he learned that a short time earlier the elder Metcalfe, after having a small boat stolen at Maui, had killed or maimed over a hundred of the islanders. He had fired his ship's guns into a mass of canoes that came out to trade with him. This piece of brutality went down in Hawaiian history as the "Olowalu massacre," from the name of the village where it took place. Kamehameha had the *Fair American* tied up in an inlet, but Metcalfe never returned to claim it.

There was a bright side to this unfortunate affair. Two English sailors from the *Fair American*, John Young and Isaac Davis, had escaped death and stayed on Hawaii.

Kamehameha had never given up his desire to have intelligent foreigners settle in his kingdom, never since those days when he had tried to persuade Lieutenant King to remain. It did not take long to convince him that Young and Davis were the type he wanted. They were practical men who understood the foreign methods of working and the use of tools. Besides, they were mature and sensible—Young was forty-six and Davis ten years younger. They would be able to explain how things were done in those lands beyond the sea. Kamehameha proposed that they should become his counselors, each with rank of chief and a generous grant of estates and servants.

This was rising in the world indeed for the two humble sailors, but at first they were not sure they would like the life. They soon fell under the spell of the hearty, ambitious Hawaiian king, however, and decided to spend their lives in his service. John Young was dubbed "Olohana" from his boatswain's cry, "All hands." Isaac Davis became "Ikake." As chiefs of the realm they married Hawaiian wives and settled down on their estates. Young married Kamehameha's niece, and one of his granddaughters became the Hawaiian Queen Emma.

Four years after he entered Kamehameha's service, John Young was asked by the explorer George Vancouver whether he would not like to return to England. He replied, "I have become used to this life of ease and tranquillity. I have no wish to launch once more into the busy world where I could earn only a bare living by hard labor."

Vancouver saw the point, but he knew that the two adopted Hawaiians were leading anything but idle lives. "I am convinced," he wrote in his journal, "that through the uniformity of their conduct and unremitting good advice to Tamaahmaah [Vancouver's spelling] and the different chiefs, they have been materially instrumental in causing the honest, civil, and attentive behavior lately experienced by all visitors from the inhabitants of this island."

CHAPTER 9

The Gods Fight for Kamehameha

KAMEHAMEHA's strongest rival for the leadership of the Hawaiian Islands was Kahekili the Thunderer of Maui. He was a dangerous enemy. He had thrown back the best that Kalaniopuu had sent against him, and he never overlooked an opportunity of stirring up trouble for his rival to the south.

He was powerful. In one way or other he controlled all the islands except Hawaii. He had been quiet for the past few years. But Kamehameha had no doubt that he was only waiting for an opening to attempt the conquest of the last and richest island of them all. There was only one sensible way to meet the threat—attack first.

In the summer of 1790, spies reported that Kahekili had gone to Oahu to enjoy the ease and pleasures of life at Waikiki, leaving the defense of Maui to his son, Kalanikupule.

Kamehameha decided that his chance had come. He had

collected a good supply of guns and ammunition from foreign traders, and he had the *Fair American* to use as the backbone of an invasion fleet. He had made peace with Keawe, the Hilo chief, who was now ready to lend him reinforcements. Kaiana, a great leader on the battlefield in spite of his unreliable character, had thrown in his lot with him. And best of all he had as advisers the Englishmen John Young and Isaac Davis, who were clever in the superior European methods of warfare.

With a huge fleet of war canoes Kamehameha descended on Maui. The outcome of the campaign was not long in doubt. The young Maui prince led his forces bravely, but he was no match for the experienced generalship and determination of Kamehameha. He was caught by surprise, and his warriors were soon driven back into a narrow valley. There Kamehameha's men cut them down mercilessly, until the stream that ran through the valley was choked with their bodies. Ever after, the battle was known as "The Damming of the Waters."

Kalanikupule escaped into the mountain forests with a few of his men. He was able to reach the seacoast and carry the news of the disaster to his father at Waikiki.

After occupying the neighboring islands of Lanai and Molokai, which offered little resistance, Kamehameha saw no reason for stopping at that point. Why not go on to a clean sweep of the rest of the islands?

He sent off a messenger to Oahu in a swift canoe bearing a flag of white tapa cloth as a sign of truce. When the envoy was ushered into the presence of Kahekili, he advanced holding both his hands out in front of him. In one hand was a small white bowling stone; in the other, a black one. It was a traditional form of ultimatum. The king was to choose either the white stone of submission or the black stone of war. But Kahekili did not care to take either one of them just then. He returned both to Kamehameha with a message.

"Wait until the black tapa covers me in death," he replied. "Then you can be the bowling stone that rolls through all the islands. Then you may take my kingdom."

Kamehameha had sent another messenger all the way to Kauai. There he secretly sought out a famous soothsayer, the wisest in all the islands.

"How," he asked, "can my king, Kamehameha, secure the help of the gods to make himself the master of all Hawaii?"

The kahuna sacrificed a pig and carefully studied its entrails. Then he examined the shapes of the clouds sailing across the sky.

"Tell your king to return to his own lands," was his advice. "Tell him to build a great new heiau at Kawaihae and dedicate it to his war god, Kukailimoku."

When the message of the soothsayer was delivered to him, Kamehameha was thinking over Kahekili's reply to his ultimatum. What course would be best? Certainly the oracle's reference to the war god implied that he would have to fight to achieve his aim. Would it not be better to strike at Oahu now, while Kahekili was rocking from the recent defeats? To build a heiau of the size and splendor that seemed called for would take much time and labor. Kamehameha was not given long to puzzle over his problem. It was solved for him suddenly by bad news from Hawaii.

Keoua of the Scarlet Cloak, brother of the late king Kiwalao and chief of Kau province, was on the warpath. He had learned of the soldiers that his uncle Keawe had sent to help Kamehameha, and he naturally resented this about-face on the part of his former ally. As soon as the army of West Hawaii was safely off to Maui, Keoua had marched into Hilo, defeated Keawe, and burned his body as a sacrifice. Now he was on the rampage in Kamehameha's territory, burning the grass villages and destroying the crops.

Kamehameha hurriedly bundled his army into their canoes and made for Hawaii. Not an hour was wasted. As soon as the warriors landed they formed up on the beaches and marched to meet the invaders. Two battles were fought, but neither side could win a decisive victory. The result was that the commanders agreed on a truce. Keoua and his men set out southward for their home in Kau, passing through Hilo to arrange for the governing of that conquered province.

And now Kamehameha remembered the advice of the soothsayer and ordered work started on the new temple. It is Kukailimoku to whom I must look for help, he reflected. I will build such a *heiau* as will place the god under great obligation.

The priests chose a site on a hillside near Kawaihae and drew up plans for the largest building project that had ever been undertaken in the islands. They designed a great platform of stone over two hundred feet long and one hundred wide. It was to be built up of terraces at various levels and surrounded on the landward side by a twenty-foot wall.

The entire population of Kamehameha's domain was mobilized to complete the work as quickly as possible. The various districts took turns sending working parties for stated periods. Whole families of workers, summoned by their feudal overlords, poured into Kawaihae and covered the near-by hillsides with their huts.

At every stage of the construction the priests sang sacred chants and performed appropriate rituals so that the work would be completely acceptable to Ku. First the ground had to be cleared and leveled. Then innumerable large stones for the walls and platforms must be carried up from the shore or rolled down from the mountainside.

It was backbreaking and uncongenial work for people whose usual building materials were poles and leaves, but who could complain when the king himself labored like any one of them? Kamehameha was not content to sit under a sunshade watching the progress of the work. Wearing only his malo and grimy with dust and sweat, he lugged stones as though the entire project depended on his personal exertions. The building of a temple was holy work, and much mana would accrue to any man who took part in it.

One blazing hot morning Kamehameha had just thrown down a stone for the masons and paused to flick the sweat from his face, when a runner approached and prostrated himself.

"O king!" he gasped, too breathless to speak distinctly. "Pele—Pele is with you!"

"Stand up," said the king, "and get enough wind so that I can understand your words."

He recognized the man as one of the spies he had sent to watch the movements of Keoua. After the runner had been given some water he made his report:

"As you ordered, your Majesty, I followed Keoua and his people when they left Hilo. All the first day I trailed them and watched from the hillsides, and all the second. The second night they made camp near the volcano Kilauea. Just after I lay down under some bushes I felt the earth begin to shake. It was the volcano goddess Pele, O king. She was more angry than any of us have ever before seen her."

Kamehameha interrupted him. "Yes, yes, we know. We felt the earth shake here and saw the fire in the sky. But Keoua?"

The man went on as though he had never been stopped. He had no intention of leaving out a single terrifying detail.

"Pele was spitting flames and smoke out the top of Kilauea, and stones and burning ashes, too. And her breath was hot and choking in my throat. Keoua's warriors and the women and children were running about shouting and screaming and not knowing which way to go. I was frightened, too. I thought——"

"Never mind your fears," shouted Kamehameha. "You are safe here now. What happened to Keoua's people?"

"All the rest of the night they ran about in confusion. Pele groaned and swore and blew out smoke. When daylight came

I saw Keoua divide the people into three groups, about four hundred in each. Then they started around the volcano, one group at a time, through the valley between Kilauea and Mauna Loa. The first division got by safely. But just after the second one set out, Pele gave a terrible roar. Rocks and hot ashes flew high into the air, even to where I was, and so much black smoke that I could see nothing over by the volcano."

Kamehameha's teeth were clenched with impatience, but he knew it would be useless to say anything.

"Then Pele's angry fit wore off," the runner continued. "I could hear her still rumbling and see her blowing out a little smoke as though she were exhausted and panting. I looked down in the valley, and there were all the people of Keoua's second division dead. They were lying with their hands grasping their throats and their legs still bent for running. Pele had burned them and hit them with stones and poisoned them with her breath."

"Did you see Keoua?" asked the king.

"Yes, your Majesty. He had stayed with the last group and escaped. He ordered the rest of his followers to start out immediately, and I saw them hurrying off into Kau."

For a moment there was silence among the workers who had gathered to listen to the story. Then the high priest stepped forward and proclaimed in a loud exultant voice:

"It is a sign, O king and chiefs! The gods are on our side! Our toil on this new *heiau* is already bearing fruit!"

His words expressed what was in everyone's mind. The

workmen went back to their stone lifting with renewed strength and enthusiasm.

Much as Kamehameha rushed the construction of his temple, he was not able to finish it before fighting another war. Kahekili may have heard of what his rival was doing. He may have decided not to wait until his enemy had completed the *heiau* and gained more favor from the war god by holding ceremonies in it.

At any rate, early in 1791 he and his brother, who was king of Kauai, launched a campaign to recapture the islands they had lost a few months before. It was a repetition of that story in reverse. The allies surprised and overwhelmed Kamehameha's garrisons on Maui and Molokai, and then turned their raiding canoes against the north coast of Hawaii itself.

Kamehameha knew that they would not stop at mere raids. They must be met and defeated. But he did not want to be forced into a full-scale war until he had finished the *heiau*. John Young suggested a naval battle. If Kahekili's canoes were destroyed he could not invade Hawaii. This was not the sort of fighting Kamehameha knew best, but he saw the wisdom of the idea and began his preparations.

In Kawaihae Bay he assembled a fleet of his swiftest war canoes. Many of them were enormous *peleleus*—two canoes, sixty or seventy feet long, joined side by side by a platform. Olohana and Ikake turned several of these into very effective gunboats by mounting Kamehameha's foreign cannon on the platforms. The flagship of the fleet was the *Fair American,* from which the king directed operations like any admiral. He waited in Kawaihae Bay until his scouts reported that the Maui war canoes were out in full force. Then he led his fleet around the north point of Hawaii and fell on the enemy in the broad channel between the two islands.

Kahekili was not expecting this flotilla that came swooping down upon him. But he, too, had some guns, and the battle was savage and bloody beyond anything those brown warriors had ever seen. Kamehameha's gunboats, divided into two squadrons to fall simultaneously upon the enemy's flanks, led the attack. When they were within range they opened a merciless cross fire.

The Englishmen had mounted the guns low and level so that the balls would skip across the water. Nearly every shot found a mark. Some cannonballs plowed through three or four canoes before spending their force. The occupants were killed outright or spilled into the water to be speared or clubbed to death when Kamehameha's men closed in for hand-to-hand combat.

The battle soon became confused. Canoes rammed one another and were grappled, so that the warriors could fight with war clubs and knives. The air was filled with shouts and screams, the splintering of wood, the booming of cannon, and the crackle of muskets. Clouds of acrid smoke obscured the bright sunshine.

From the deck of the *Fair American* Kamehameha saw many of his canoes swamped and scores of his warriors killed, but, when the sun was about halfway down the sky, the smashed

remnant of Kahekili's fleet broke away and scurried for the
Maui shore. He had won the "Battle of the Red-mouthed
Guns." Hawaii was safe. Although he had not been able to
hold his conquests of a year before, he had dealt Kahekili a
body blow that would keep him quiet for some time to come.

The last stone of the great *heiau* was laid in place in the
fall of 1791, and the temple was consecrated with the most
solemn ceremonies. Kamehameha was a devout man whose
faith in the power of the gods was firm and strong. He believed, too, that they were inclined to look with favor upon
his plans for uniting the islands. As he proudly surveyed this
towering token of his reverence for them, he was confident
that he could move forward assured of divine good will.

The events of the past year had taught Kamehameha that
his first task must be to make secure his position on Hawaii. It
would be folly to turn his face again toward the other islands
while the hostile districts of Hawaii remained poised like a
dagger at his back. In a way, the problem was simpler than it
had been a year ago. Then there were two rivals to deal with;
now there was only one—Keoua of the Scarlet Cloak, who had
escaped the wrath of the volcano.

One of Kamehameha's most remarkable traits was his ability
to profit by past experience. His success in making an ally of
the late Keawe of Hilo had shown him that diplomacy and
peaceful means can sometimes accomplish more than force.

At this stage of his career Kamehameha no longer loved war
for the mere sake of fighting. He had progressed beyond the
old ideals of Alapai and Kalaniopuu, who had never been happy

unless they were leading their warriors into battle. He had a nobler vision: the chain of beautiful islands united under one monarch, free from internal strife and strong to meet the ever more numerous visitors fron the outside world.

The soothsayer of Kauai, it was true, had told him to look to the bloodthirsty god Kukailimoku as his patron. But perhaps some of the dream could be realized by less violent means. He invited Keoua of the Scarlet Cloak up to Kawaihae to see if they could end their nine-year-old dispute. If this method failed, Kamehameha reflected, he could always lead his army into Kau and force a settlement.

Keoua accepted the invitation and went with the envoys to Kamehameha's court. He knew that the parley would strip him of his power. His ambitious cousin would never agree to any settlement that did not leave him master of the whole island. But what was the alternative? His own people were convinced that it was futile to resist the king of West Hawaii. The disaster on the slopes of Kilauea had been a tremendous blow to their morale.

"The gods are against us," they said. "The gods fight on the side of Kamehameha."

So Keoua went to the conference, taking with him his brother and his most trusted chiefs.

When news of Keoua's arrival was brought to him, Kamehameha was in the new *heiau*. He immediately came out and shouted a greeting from the hillside. As he descended the slope he could see his guests' canoes being run in through the shallow water.

Suddenly, just as the chiefs from Kau were about to step

ashore, Keeaumoku the Kingmaker seized a short stabbing spear from a warrior and drove it deep into Keoua's side. The unlucky chieftain topped over dead into the surf. Kamehameha rushed down and was just in time to save Keoua's brother from a similar fate.

The prophecy of the Kauai seer had been fulfilled. Kamehameha was master of the whole island of Hawaii. It had not come about as he had planned it. But who can foresee, thought Kamehameha, how the gods will accomplish their designs? And he ordered the body of Keoua to be burned on the altar of the new *heiau* as a sacrifice of thanksgiving.

CHAPTER 10

My Friend Kanekupa

THE BEACH AT Kealakekua was crowded with people, all looking out across the water. They were watching the progress of a flotilla of large, black canoes that had just put out from the shore.

There were eleven altogether, and they rode low in the water as though they were heavily loaded. They moved in a perfect arrowhead formation causing the dozens of small craft that dotted the water to scurry out of their path. The point of the arrow was a tall, erect figure dressed in brilliant yellow. It was Kamehameha, standing proudly in the bow of the leading canoe, the largest of them all with eighteen paddlers on a side.

Kamehameha was going to visit two large ships that were anchored out in the bay. His scouts had reported these foreign ships coming along the coast. People from the northern part of the island had gone out to them. They were ships from

Beretanee, the scouts said, and their chief was an explorer like Kapene Kuka who had died at Kealakekua years ago.

From the deck of the larger of the ships their commander watched the approach of the canoes. His name was George Vancouver and his vessels were the sloop of war *Discovery,* named after Captain Cook's old ship, and the armed tender *Chatham.* He was under orders from the British Admiralty to survey the northwest coast of America and determine whether there was a passage from the Pacific Ocean to the Great Lakes.

Fourteen years earlier, Vancouver had been at Kealakekua as a midshipman under Captain Cook. Now, on this February day of 1793, the scene brought back sad memories as he studied the shoreline. There was the village of Kekua and near it the dark bulk of the *heiau.* Extending northward was the steep face of the cliff, and there beside the large rock was the very place where Captain Cook had been killed.

For a moment Vancouver was again a twenty-year-old middy watching from the deck of an older *Discovery* the scuffle that had cost the life of the great navigator. Now in a similar expedition, the responsibility of command was his. On this occasion, he hoped the outcome would be more fortunate.

By this time Kamehameha's flotilla had reached the English ships. With the paddlers keeping perfect time, the canoes executed a series of maneuvers, following the signaled orders of the king. Suddenly the ten canoes loaded with provisions drew up in line under the *Discovery's* stern, and the one bearing the king shot forward along the ship's starboard side. When Kamehameha was exactly opposite the ladder, the canoe was instantly and skillfully brought to a dead stop. The sailors were filled with admiration by this display of Hawaiian seamanship.

Vancouver had anticipated this formal visit. When Kamehameha stepped on deck to the twittering of the bosuns' pipes, the captain and his officers, all in full uniform, stood ready to greet him. The noble figure of the king in his red and yellow feather helmet and yellow feather cloak, open in front and revealing his athletic brown body, made a striking contrast against the blue and gold of the Royal Navy.

"Aloha!" said Kamehameha warmly.

Then, grasping Vancouver's hand, he asked simply and seriously, as though he would be completely bound by the answer, "I am told that your name is Kanekupa. Are you sincerely my friend?"

The captain caught the mood and answered in one word, "Yes."

"I understand," the king continued, "that you belong to King George. Is he also my friend?"

"Yes," repeated Vancouver.

"Then," said Kamehameha, "I am your firm, good friend. You and your people are welcome to my island of Hawaii."

The two men then touched noses in the Hawaiian manner. Any uncertainty Vancouver might have had about Kamehameha's attitude toward the expedition was completely dispelled. He felt strongly attached to this straightforward, intelligent island king, and he could easily see that his feelings were reciprocated.

Vancouver recognized Kamehameha readily, but he was agreeably surprised to see the change that fourteen years had made. He had expected to know the king by his hard, savage countenance. Instead, he found that the years had softened Kamehameha's ferocity of face and had given him, as Vancouver wrote in his journal, "an address characteristic of an open, cheerful, and sensible mind; combined with great generosity and goodness of spirit."

Kamehameha was beside himself with excitement and good nature. He asked if some of his family and courtiers might come aboard, then ran eagerly to the rail to shout at the bobbing canoes.

The first to step on deck was a tall, stately girl who immediately walked over to Kamehameha. This was his favorite wife whom he had married just recently. She was the daughter of "the kingmaker," Keeaumoku, and had the comfortable, wifely name of Kaahumanu, "The Cloak of Feathers." This had been no marriage to secure an alliance with a powerful chief; it was a love match on both sides. Beautiful and intelligent, Kaahumanu was born to be a queen.

Kamehameha took his pretty young wife by the hand and led her up to Vancouver. She made an immediate conquest of him and everyone else on deck by taking a fragrant flower lei from her neck and throwing it over the captain's shoulders.

"And now, Kanekupa," said the king, "I have brought you and your men some provisions as a gift from me. May my people carry them on board?"

The *Discovery's* petty officers quickly detailed men to rig booms and hoisting nets. Kamehameha had brought provisions enough for a squadron. Fat hogs by the dozen came up over the side until there were nearly a hundred of them grunting and squealing on the deck. Nets full of vegetables and fruits and coconuts spilled out their contents into huge piles.

Then, to Vancouver's consternation, a canoeload of plump dogs was hauled aboard. The sailors stared in openmouthed astonishment. Kamehameha, seeing the captain's bewildered expression, went over to him.

"Kanekupa, do you not like the dogs?"

"Yes, I like dogs," Vancouver explained. "But I have never eaten one."

"Oh, but they taste fine," the king urged. "You roast them just like the pigs."

"But in my country," explained Vancouver, "we keep dogs as pets. They became almost like members of the family."

Kamehameha reflected a moment on the strange ways of the foreigners. "But, Kanekupa, don't you get tired of eating pig, pig, pig all the time?"

Vancouver made no answer but smiled mysteriously and gave an order to one of his officers. In a few minutes half a dozen sailors appeared leading several animals from their pens on the afterdeck. There were five lumbering cows, three ewes, and a rather wicked-looking ram. Now it was the Hawaiian's turn to be astonished.

"What are they?" he asked.

"These are what we eat as a change from pig," Vancouver told him. "The small ones are sheep, male and female. The big ones are cows, and we call their meat beef."

"Hipa—pipi," said Kamehameha, imitating "sheep" and "beef" as best he could. He examined the cows carefully. "These five all seem to be pipi *wahines*," he said. "Have you no pipi *kane?*"

"Yes," answered Vancouver. "Keeaumoku's people are taking care of a bull. It became sick a few days ago and I had to put it ashore up at Kawaihae. But all of them are for you."

Kamehameha was delighted with these wonderful new animals and asked to be told how to take care of them. The ship's cook was called up to explain their feeding and to demonstrate the process of milking the cows. While the cattle were being loaded into canoes for the trip ashore, the king hovered and fussed about like a mother hen lest any accident should befall them. He watched anxiously from the deck until he saw them standing safe and sound on the beach.

Kamehameha was sorely tempted to roast just one of these delicacies, but his good sense won out. Vancouver suggested placing a ten-year tabu on the animals, and the king named a lush, secluded valley where they might graze and multiply unhindered. In 1815 Kamehameha gave the descendants of these cattle into the charge of John Parker, a sailor from Newton, Massachusetts. This New Englander married and settled permanently on Hawaii and became the founder of the huge Parker ranch, one of the largest in the world.

The Hawaiians were led below to the *Discovery's* cabin for

refreshments. Kamehameha realized his ignorance of European etiquette, but he was determined to do the proper thing if possible. He gravely asked Vancouver if he might sit down and which chair he should take.

When all were comfortable, the captain announced that he had some presents for them. Kamehameha immediately arose and said he would like to take charge of the distribution. He knew the relative rank and merit of his people, he said, and would make sure none of these precious gifts from so far beyond the seas were wasted. He stood beside the open chest like a Polynesian Santa Claus and called his courtiers up one at a time.

But he was determined not to dig too deeply into the treasure chest of this generous captain. He doled out the presents so sparingly, in fact, that Vancouver laughingly took a position beside him and added something to each of the king's gifts. Kamehameha gave him a look that seemed to say, "What a foolish waste!"—especially when the captain heaped presents on the women. This caused a great deal of merriment, and no one laughed louder than the king himself.

And now it was time for Kamehameha's present. While the Hawaiians watched eagerly to see what their king would get, Vancouver opened a locker and took out a bright scarlet cloak. He draped it about his guest's broad shoulders and had looking glasses placed opposite each other. The cloak reached to the deck and was rather gaudy; it was trimmed with gold lace and tied down the front with blue ribbons.

Vancouver had chosen well. Kamehameha was as pleased as

a boy. He strutted and capered about, so that those who were nearest the door of the crowded cabin were forced out to make room for him. Throwing the captain a look of gratitude, he went out on deck. For several minutes, assuming an air of casualness, he paraded near the rail. The ship was now surrounded by canoes full of islanders. Hundreds more, both men and women, were in the water, many of them holding in one hand a small pig or a fowl that they hoped to exchange for a trinket. The people shouted their admiration, the king beamed his pleasure, and again Vancouver marveled at the simple naturalness with which these islanders displayed their emotions.

By this time Kamehameha was sure that Vancouver had no unfriendly intentions toward Hawaii. He was determined that no unpleasantness should develop if he could prevent it.

"Kanekupa," he suggested, "we are all friends, of course. But sometimes people misunderstand one another, and then there is trouble. I think it would be a good idea if you and I made some rules that all our people would know and obey."

Vancouver readily agreed and suggested holding a council of chiefs and officers in the cabin. He was impressed and agreeably surprised by the good sense and intelligence of the Hawaiian king.

The joint council met and agreed on several basic rules for the conduct of the two groups toward each other. The sailors were to refrain from trespassing in the *heiaus* and were to treat with respect all sacred things. They were not to wander about the country unless they obtained Kamehameha's permission and were accompanied by a guide. Only the principal chiefs were to be admitted to the English ships. Any offense on the part of the islanders was to be reported to Kamehameha for punishment.

The king asked also that two of his canoes be allowed to patrol all night around the ships as guard boats. Vancouver objected to this proposal, fearing that the Hawaiians might think his men could not take care of themselves. But Kamehameha thought it a good precaution, and that night sent out the two canoes in spite of Vancouver's objection. The watch officer on the *Discovery*, hearing the paddling in the darkness, became alarmed and ordered out a launch to row guard. Next morning it was learned that the ships had been guarding themselves against canoes assigned to protect them, and from then on the king had his way.

CHAPTER II

A Present for George III

WHILE THE *Discovery* and the *Chatham* lay in Kealakekua Bay, Kamehameha devoted his whole time to helping the explorers with their work and making their visit pleasant. He gave Vancouver permission to set up his observatory tents and instruments on the same spot used by Captain Cook fourteen years earlier.

The fresh water supply at Kealakekua had fallen low, and filling the ships' water casks presented something of a problem. Kamehameha solved it by ordering a number of his canoes to take the barrels to various parts of the coast and fill them from wells on the near-by farms. He set as fair payment for the men a piece of iron six inches long and two inches wide for each cask filled.

One of the most colorful events of the visit occurred when Kamehameha invited Vancouver to accompany him on a formal Sunday promenade through the district.

The English officers and a guard of marines, wearing their

best dress uniforms, were met by the king and a group of his chiefs. All the Hawaiians wore their brilliant ceremonial feather capes and helmets except Kamehameha. He was resplendent in his gift from Vancouver, the scarlet cloak trimmed with gold lace, which he was wearing officially for the first time.

The party made a stately tour of the villages that lay around the bay. All along the route were crowds of gaping islanders, exclaiming in admiration at the display of color and the gorgeous figure of their king. As they paraded in the bright sunshine or through the cool green shade of the trees, Kamehameha was at the height of his glory.

They visited the royal palace. It consisted of three main buildings surrounded by a stone wall. The largest, and the only one the party entered, was the king's daytime dwelling and royal council chamber. It was a well-proportioned, thatched building about thirty feet long. The interior was very plain. Around the walls stood a low divan covered, like the floor, with *lauhala* mats. The other two buildings in the enclosure were a dwelling for the women and the sleeping house of the king and queen.

When they came to the spot where Captain Cook had been killed, the chiefs became very solemn. They told their guests how deeply they deplored that unfortunate tragedy. They all seemed to look on it, however, as something that had been bound to happen.

One priest explained that after the desecration of the *heiau* the *kahunas*, who could see the intentions of the gods, had foretold the death of Cook. It was true, he said, that the chiefs had consented to the removal of the fence and images, but that made no difference to the gods. And any prophecy of the *kahunas* was likely to come true or, as the priest implied, be made to come true.

Kamehameha saw one of the Englishmen pick up a stone from the beach.

"Why do you take the stone?" he asked.

The man explained that he wanted it to take home as a souvenir from the place where Cook had died.

Kamehameha snatched the stone from his hand and threw it into the sea.

"If you took that back," he said, "it would only revive the memory of an unhappy event. After reconciliation, people should not reopen old sores."

Kamehameha spent as much time as possible on the *Discovery*, often turning up in time for breakfast. He walked all over the ship from stem to stern, curiously watching one operation after another and asking a constant stream of questions. Why must the iron be made so hot before it is hammered? What are the sails made of? How far can this cannon throw a shot?

His eye was always on the lookout for devices and tools and methods that he thought he could put to good use. These sailors knew things that he and his people had never dreamed of. He knew that Beretanee was Beretanee and Hawaii was Hawaii. He had no wish to see his countrymen chasing after every foreign custom. But if a sharp piece of iron shapes a canoe more quickly than a sharp piece of stone, why not use it?

The king was a lover of good food, and his burly, active body required huge quantities of fuel. Thomas Manby, the master's mate on the *Chatham*, once watched him make away with a dog, two large fish, and an enormous calabash of poi. And so two parts of the ship that Kamehameha found especially interesting were the galley and the table in the captain's cabin. The meals he ate on board were so much to his taste, in fact, that he brought along his own personal chef to learn English cooking. And before the ships left he got from each of them a knife, a fork, and a plate.

"Now," he said, "I can eat the way George does."

One afternoon Kamehameha took Vancouver and his men to watch one of his favorite amusements, a sham battle. A large crowd would be on hand, he said, and would Kanekupa bring along the guard of marines in their bright scarlet coats? No guards were in fact needed; the request sprang from the king's love of pageantry and his own personal vanity. He loved to be the center of a colorful ceremony.

The battle was between two companies of warriors representing Hawaii and Maui. It was a wild affair, with both sides yelling defiance and casting spears at one another—blunted, but still capable of giving painful wounds. The crowd shouted and cheered. One group rooted for the Maui team, not because they were unpatriotic, but because their favorite warriors happened to be on that side.

Kamehameha himself took part for a short time and astonished the Englishmen with his skill. Six spears were hurled at him at the same time. He caught three of them in his right hand as they were flying through the air, broke two others by parrying them with his own spear held in his left hand, and dodged the sixth.

The battle ended when the chiefs impersonating the Maui leaders were declared killed. These unfortunate fellows were dragged by the heels over the beach and presented to Kamehameha to be "sacrificed." Their ears and noses and mouths were full of sand, but they took it all with good humor and ran into the sea to wash themselves.

One of Vancouver's dearest hopes was to be able to persuade these island people whom he liked so well to live together in peace. It seemed to him that the only cause of their fighting was a greedy ambition to seize one another's lands. This meant constant warfare, for, when a piece of land was taken, it was soon recaptured and changed hands continually.

Aside from the actual ravages of battle, the land suffered from neglect. The men were forced to spend their time bearing arms instead of cultivating the fields, and food became scarce. And, if this waste continued, the usefulness of the islands as a source of supplies for American and European traders would be seriously impaired.

Looking down the years, Vancouver could see the island harbors filled with ships of the China and Northwest Coast trade, making the Hawaiians prosperous by their purchase of provisions. At the same time, these friendly brown people would steadily improve their condition by adopting the tools and methods of more advanced countries.

The greatest obstacle in the way of peace was a mutual, deep distrust. Kamehameha feared that any agreement they made would soon be broken by his old enemy Kahekili. The only way to secure permanent peace, he told Vancouver, was to conquer, once and for all, the powerful ruler of Maui.

What the Hawaiians really wanted was the assistance of the English ships and guns in a new attempt against the westward islands. It was strong evidence of the friendship Kamehameha and Vancouver held for each other that the captain's firm refusal caused no ill feeling between them.

Vancouver made a brief visit to Maui, where he heard the same argument against peace. They did not trust the enemy. If a treaty were made, said King Kahekili, the chiefs who were now on Maui for their mutual protection would return to their own islands. Then Kamehameha and his warriors would swoop down. The explorer reluctantly decided that he was wasting his time in the role of peacemaker.

On Tuesday morning, March 5, 1793, Vancouver told Kamehameha that he planned to leave within a day or so. Keenly disappointed that his friends could not stay longer, the king went out to the *Discovery* with his farewell presents. To Vancouver he gave a collection of native curiosities and a handsome feather cape.

Far outshining this, however, was a gift entrusted to the captain to be delivered to King George III. It was the gorgeous yellow feather cloak that Kamehameha had worn on his formal visit, the cloak that had been started at Awini before he was born. It was the finest ever made in the islands. He proudly spread it out to display its beauty and pointed to two jagged holes that had been torn through it.

"Those," said Kamehameha, "are places where enemy spears were thrust at me the first time I wore it in battle. They tore the cloak—and my skin, too. My skin has healed up, but I have never let the holes in the cloak be mended. No one but me has ever worn it, Kanekupa. I want you to promise not to let anyone put it on before you give it to George. It is the most valuable thing in Hawaii."

He folded the cloak carefully and handed it to Vancouver. It was as though King George were to send the crown jewels to another monarch as a token of friendship.

Vancouver was deeply impressed and gladly made the required promise. In return he gave the king a generous gift of cooking utensils and blacksmith's and carpenter's tools. Beaming with good will and affection, Kamehameha then said good-by to the officers and to every sailor he saw on the deck.

Next morning the ships had not yet sailed because of a heavy swell that was running into the bay. The islanders were delighted and came swarming out in their canoes. Vancouver wondered why Kamehameha, usually among the first arrivals, was not to be seen. But the reason for his delay was soon clear.

A few days earlier, Vancouver had ordered his men to rig one of the large royal canoes with a set of sails. The king was very proud of this craft and now, waiting until the most dramatic moment, he came sailing out in state. When he boarded the *Discovery*, Kamehameha had a shrewd gleam in his eye.

"Kanekupa," he asked, "what kind of warship did you say has sails set up like mine?"

"A sloop."

"Ah, yes—a sloop. You know, Kanekupa, my sloop would

look a lot more like one of George's if it had one thing."

"What is that, sir?" asked Vancouver. He guessed what the answer would be.

"A few of those little swivel guns you have."

"Yes," the captain agreed, "they would make it look more warlike. But they are all tabu to King George."

For a man who observed the laws of tabu as strictly as Kamehameha did, that settled the matter.

Kamehameha told Vancouver that he would like to ride up the coast a way on the *Discovery,* but his religion required him to perform a purification ceremony immediately. He had taken food and drink with the English officers, and they were men who had sat at the same table with women. The two gentlemen then said a final "Aloha," and Vancouver promised to return after he had visited the coast of America.

The coming of Vancouver's ships had been very welcome to Kamehameha. The seizure of the *Fair American* had given the islands a bad name among merchant skippers. Some of them had wrongly placed the blame on Kamehameha. He wanted a chance to show his true self to an important foreigner and contradict the bad reports that had been circulated. He must have realized, when the English captain sailed away, that he had been successful. Not only had he convinced Vancouver of his good will, he had made a warm, personal friend.

CHAPTER 12

The King Plays a Trick

KAMEHAMEHA WAS LIVING at Hilo on the windward side of Hawaii when Vancouver returned to the islands in January 1794. As luck would have it, Vancouver had selected that very spot for his first port of call. He wanted to see how the harbor compared with Kealakekua Bay. The king was overjoyed at seeing his friend once more, especially at Hilo, which was one of his favorite parts of the island. He hoped Vancouver would make a long stay there.

But at breakfast, a meal Kamehameha always enjoyed aboard the ship, the captain explained that the trade winds and the heavy seas that ran into the harbor at that time of year made Hilo too risky an anchorage. He said he must continue on to Kealakekua and asked the king to accompany him.

Kamehameha regretted that he could not very well do this, at least not for several days. It was the *makahiki* season, he explained, and a tabu obliged him to remain for a certain time in the district where he had begun the festival.

Vancouver was disappointed. He wanted to leave immediately, and he wanted the king to go with him. In spite of his very friendly reception last year, he felt uneasy. Kamehameha's company would be a welcome insurance against unpleasant incidents. This seemed so important to Vancouver that he took a rather unfair advantage of the king's warm and generous nature.

"I see," he said, assuming an injured look, "that you no longer feel as friendly toward me as a year ago. I thought I could always count on your friendship. But then, I suppose, there are few things that time cannot change."

Kamehameha laid down his knife and pushed away his plate. For a minute he sat without speaking. He was deeply hurt. Finally he said, "I will go with you. The king should be the last one to break the laws of his people. But perhaps it is more important to show you that Kamehameha does not lightly change his friends each year."

He then sent a chief ashore to tell the priests his intention and ask their indulgence. Seven chiefs had accompanied the king aboard, some of them with their wives. They now crowded around to assure him that he was doing the right thing. They were as eager as children for a ride on the great ship.

When Kamehameha had first come aboard, Vancouver had noticed with surprise that Kaahumanu was not with him. The year before, she had always accompanied the king on his visits to the *Discovery*. Her good looks and liveliness and intelligence had made her a favorite with everyone on the ship.

Vancouver took aside one of the chiefs and learned that the royal couple had quarreled. The king had accused Kaahumanu of being too friendly with the handsome Kaiana, and she had gone home to her parents. Vancouver asked Kamehameha whether he could be of any help in bringing about a reconciliation, but he met with a firm rebuff.

"Kanekupa," said the king haughtily, "in my public matters I am proud to receive your help, but I am able to settle my private troubles alone."

Vancouver wisely resolved to wait for a more favorable opportunity. It came one evening while he and the king were sitting at the cabin table over a bottle of port wine.

"That was a good dinner, Kanekupa," said Kamehameha, "and this wine is good, too."

"Yes," remarked the captain casually. "Only one thing is lacking to make this a real banquet."

"What is that?"

"A beautiful woman to join us afterward."

For a moment Kamehameha was silent. Then he answered, "You think it is foolish to continue this quarrel with Kaahumanu. I also think it is foolish. But I do not know how to end it. I cannot be the first to seek forgiveness."

"No, I suppose not." Vancouver tried not to smile. "Why not ask one of your chiefs to be your go-between?"

"I cannot ask them now. I told them it was not their business."

"Well, then," said the captain, "do you think that I could help?"

Kamehameha jumped up and grasped his friend's hand gratefully.

Vancouver was equally pleased. He had a deep affection for the royal couple and wished to see them happy. And more than that, he feared that if the separation were continued it might prove a real danger to Kamehameha's authority and the peace of his kingdom.

Vancouver had talked with Kaahumanu's father and knew that the old chief was mightily displeased. He and other members of the family had tried to bring the couple together, but one was as proud and stubborn as the other. The quarrel had been caused by idle gossip and lies. Kamehameha should have had more sense than to believe them. The chief expressed himself so strongly that Vancouver feared the affair might end in a family feud.

Kamehameha and Vancouver put their heads together to work out a plan. The king insisted that no one must know he had taken any part in the scheme. He wished the whole thing to appear to be accidental, for he was not sure how the queen felt about making up the quarrel.

They finally decided that Vancouver should invite Kaahumanu on board ship and find out whether she was willing to be friends with her husband. He would then send a message to the king to let him know her feelings. For the message, Kamehameha took two pieces of paper and made different pencil marks on each. The one was to be sent if the queen were in a forgiving mood, the other if she proved stubborn.

Everything worked out perfectly. When Kaahumanu came aboard, greatly pleased by the invitation, Vancouver made no mention of the quarrel. He distributed some small presents to her and her ladies, and then suggested they send something to the king as a joke. Kaahumanu was delighted at the idea. Vancouver wrapped the piece of paper that meant "yes" carefully in tapa cloth and sent it ashore to Kamehameha.

The king, of course, was waiting for it eagerly and immediately had himself paddled out to the ship. The group in the cabin heard him coming across the deck. He was calling to Vancouver and thanking him in an assumed sarcastic voice for the valuable present.

At the sound of her husband's voice, Kaahumanu was overcome with surprise and agitation. The other girls tittered with excitement. Kamehameha played his part well. He came bursting into the cabin, saw Kaahumanu, and at once seemed all surprise and confusion. He made a step back as though he would leave, but Vancouver took his hand and joined it with that of the queen.

With tears of joy running down their cheeks, the couple threw their arms about each other and embraced tenderly. In an instant all was gaiety, and Vancouver sealed the reunion by having wine served all around.

And then Vancouver was due for a surprise. When the party was ready to leave, Kaahumanu said she had a favor to ask of the captain. He must make Kamehameha promise not to be angry and not to beat her when they got home! Vancouver thought she was joking, but even after Kamehameha had said he had no intention of being angry, she insisted that the captain accompany them back to the royal residence. This he did, and was happy to see how delighted all their subjects were when the king and queen returned home together.

Kamehameha never tired of asking Vancouver and his officers about the way men lived in Beretanee and, among other things, about their religion. But certainly nothing that Vancouver or anyone else told him ever induced him to turn away from his ancient gods.

To the pagan Hawaiians religion was a practical matter. One of the guests at a dinner on the ship was a "Padre" John Howel, an adventurer who had once been a clergyman. The conversation turned to religion, and the "Padre" harangued the king on the advantages of embracing the Christian faith. Kamehameha listened patiently and then made a proposition.

"You say your God watches over those who love him, and protects them?"

"That is true," answered Howel.

"You must prove to me that what you say is true," said Kamehameha. "If I were to jump from the top of Kealakekua cliff, my gods could not save me from death. You go and do that and call upon your God to protect you. If I find you unharmed at the bottom, I will embrace the worship of your God."

"Padre" Howel decided that the Hawaiian king was not yet ready for conversion.

At one shipboard dinner Vancouver asked that the meat of

the cattle he had brought to the islands should not be made tabu to the women. Kamehameha agreed, with one reservation. No woman must eat meat from the same animal as a man.

Whenever he could find an excuse for introducing the subject, Kamehameha renewed his request for cannon and firearms. But Vancouver felt that the king had enough of an arsenal already. He did provide one weapon, however, that Kamehameha put to good use the next year in his conquest of the islands.

An English sailor named Robert Boyd, who had left the sea to enter the service of the Hawaiian king, had undertaken to build a sailing vessel. He got as far as having the timber cut, and then found himself at a loss how to start. Young and Davis tried to help, but they were as much in the dark as Boyd about laying the keel and setting up the frame properly. When Vancouver heard of the difficulty, he sent his carpenters ashore to start the construction. In a short time the outline of the vessel began to take shape. She was thirty-six feet long with a draft of five feet and was to be named the *Britannia*.

Kamehameha was fascinated by the shipbuilding. At almost any hour of the day he could be found at the shipyard watching his first modern man-of-war take form.

For three weeks the carpenters worked so diligently on the *Britannia* that what remained to be done when they left was well within the power of Boyd. To make it complete, Vancouver gave Kamehameha all the iron fittings he would need, oakum and pitch for calking the seams, and the proper masts and sails to rig the vessel schooner fashion.

CHAPTER 13

"Kanaka Beretanee"

FOR SEVERAL YEARS now Kamehameha had been trying to make up his mind on an important question of national policy. Would it not be a wise move to place his kingdom under the protection of one of the powerful foreign countries?

More and more ships were coming to the islands every year, and relations with the foreigners were not always pleasant. Too many traders looked upon the Hawaiians as ignorant savages for whom no consideration need be shown. Some of them stocked their ships with island produce and left in payment worthless trash, or even nothing at all.

Others, taking advantage of the islanders' ignorance of firearms, brought guns and pistols so cheaply constructed that they burst the first time they were fired. More than one Hawaiian had thus lost several fingers or an arm, or even his life. Gunpowder—"burning sand," as the Hawaiians called it—was often adulterated with ground charcoal. Many of these sea captains, like the murderous Captain Metcalfe, had been overbearing and cruel. Certainly, Kamehameha felt, if his people enjoyed the protection of a strong country, incidents of that sort would be less likely to happen.

He had already seen the flags of several superior nations—England, the United States, Spain—and there were still others, he knew. How long would it be until one or another of these powers would compel him to submit by force? Would it not be better to acknowledge now the supremacy of one of them and place Hawaii voluntarily under its protection?

Of all foreign visitors, the English had been the first and the most numerous. From what Kamehameha had seen of his ships, the English King George was evidently a great and strong ruler in the outside world. And no other foreigner had shown so much kindness and good will as George's Captain Vancouver. If it were wise to choose a protector, the choice seemed obvious.

He had discussed the idea more than once with Vancouver in 1793 but had made no decision then. But by the time the explorer returned, Kamehameha had convinced himself and his chiefs that a cession of Hawaii to Great Britain would be a sensible and beneficial move.

Vancouver had long since made up his mind that if the king made a formal offer of cession he would accept for the British government. He foresaw that trade in the Pacific was likely to expand greatly, in which case the islands would be of immense usefulness to his country. He also believed sincerely that an association with England would benefit these islanders in whose welfare he had come to take such an active interest. Vancouver insisted, however, that any move must be made openly and publicly agreed to by all of the chiefs. And so Kamehameha called all his principal chiefs together for a grand conference. The summons was a signal for everyone of any consequence, men and women, to take a holiday and journey to the shores of Kealakekua Bay. The high chiefs of the six districts of the island, each with a large following of friends and attendants, came one by one. It was several days before the more distant ones arrived. Crowds of curious sightseers, eager to see the English ships and share in the excitement of the gathering, soon jammed every house and temporary shelter in the neighborhood.

The days of waiting for the last chiefs to arrive were filled with visiting, renewing of old acquaintances, and all sorts of games and entertainments. Noisy *luaus,* those tremendous Hawaiian feasts, filled the air with the savory aroma of baked pig. And there was a perfect passion for games of chance. Vancouver noted that the gambling was always carried on with good temper and merriment, even on the part of the losers. Some of the more businesslike islanders came prepared to barter for tools and iron from the ships.

One afternoon was set aside for a full-dress performance of a hula in honor of the foreign guests. The leading roles were to be taken by some of the ladies of Kamehameha's court, and the king saw to it that all details were thoroughly rehearsed beforehand.

At about four o'clock Kamehameha and Kaahumanu met

Vancouver and his officers and took them to the open-air
theater. It was a square clearing shaded by tall pandanus
trees. When the royal party arrived the crowd had only just
begun to gather. But Kamehameha had planned to get there
well ahead of time. He wanted to make a last-minute, personal check of everything.

Kamehameha was considered by the performers as an absolute authority on the fine points of the hula. He bustled
about answering a question here and making a suggestion
there. The ladies even consulted him concerning their cos-
tumes. The principal garment was a large piece of fine tapa
wound about the waist and extending to the knees. This had
to be arranged carefully in elaborate pleats, a very exacting
job. As each performer finished arranging this skirt, the king
would stand back and survey her critically. And any adjust-
ment he suggested was promptly made.

Then, when all was ready, came the most disappointing part
of the whole affair for the king and queen. They had to leave
the theater, for a religious tabu forbade them to attend an
entertainment of this sort except at the celebration of the
new year. Kaahumanu was especially reluctant to leave. She
was an expert dancer and would have liked nothing better
than to take one of the parts.

By this time the theater was filled with spectators, as many
as four thousand. In the front rows on mats the chiefs and
their wives sat in corpulent dignity, attended by their fan
boys and fly chasers. Cries of "Hula! Hula!" rose from vari-

ous parts of the crowd, for it was getting late and custom required that the performance be over by sundown.

A master of ceremonies put the spectators in good humor with an introductory joke or two, and the music began. The orchestra consisted of five men, each holding a polished wooden spear in his left hand. The musicians sang and beat on their spears with short sticks, varying the tone by striking different parts of the tapered spears. The hour-long performance was a combination of speaking, singing, and dancing, all woven together in harmony to carry on the narrative.

The story in this case was that of the young princess Keopuolani, whom Kamehameha had brought back from Molokai. Her parents held the highest rank among the noble families of the islands. Years later, when Keopuolani had grown to womanhood, Kamehameha made her his "sacred wife" and she became the mother of the two sons who followed him to the throne. Her rank was so high that even when Kamehameha became lord of all the islands he had to prostrate himself when entering her presence.

The hula ended as the last rays of the sun were turning Mauna Loa's snowy cap to gold. Then Vancouver sprang a surprise that he had prepared. He signaled to a group of seamen on the edge of the crowd. Streaming tails of fire, a salvo of rockets sailed up into the evening sky and burst high over head.

The Hawaiians were terror-stricken. Some fell on their faces in dismay. Some made for the trees.

Kamehameha, probably thinking how helpless his country would be against the power the rockets represented, was heard to exclaim, "Poor Hawaii! Poor Hawaii! You are no more!"

He set off two of the fireworks himself and asked for some to frighten his enemies. Vancouver satisfied him by leaving several sky rockets and grenades with John Young, on the understanding that they were to be used only to protect the king if that should ever be necessary.

Vancouver also sent up some Bengal lights that hung glowing like full moons to light the islanders to their homes. The next day he learned that people in distant villages, seeing the fiery display in the sky, had feared the foreigners were quarreling with the king and destroying him and his warriors.

On the day of the conference Vancouver entertained Kamehameha and his chiefs at dinner in his tent on the beach. During the meal there occurred an incident that almost ended in a repetition of the Captain Cook tragedy.

One of the chiefs present was Kameeiamoku, the man who had captured the *Fair American*. Because of the seizure of the American schooner, Vancouver had refused to have anything to do with him or permit his people to trade with the ships. But with the conference drawing near, the captain had decided to set an example to the islanders by an act of forgiveness. And so the guilty chief had been invited.

All through the meal Kameeiamoku was extremely ill at ease. The other Hawaiians were in a joking mood and amused themselves by making fun of his table manners. Because of his lack of intercourse with the foreigners, the surly chief did not know how to go about attacking a European-style meal. When the brandy was served, however, Kameeiamoku resolved to show that he could drink with any of them. He had a bottle set at his place and poured himself glass after glass.

But he little knew the power of the foreign awa. Suddenly he collapsed, dead drunk. Everyone jumped up and Kameeiamoku's men carried him out into the open air. As he passed Vancouver he gave the captain a look of savage hatred, and muttered with his tongue lolling helplessly out of his mouth that he had been poisoned.

His friends immediately became hostile and threatening. One of them drew an iron dagger from his malo. Kamehameha jumped forward and explained the real cause of Kameeiamoku's discomfort. But the man with the dagger shouted angrily that his master had been given a different bottle to drink from.

Kamehameha instantly stepped to the drunken chief's vacant place, poured a glass of brandy from the bottle in question, and drank it down. The man with the dagger was satisfied, and Vancouver breathed a sigh of relief.

At the conference that followed, Kamehameha insisted that if he ceded the island to Britain no change would be made in the government or religion of Hawaii. The local authority of himself, his chiefs, and the priests was to remain undisturbed. This was agreed to, and the chiefs declared themselves "kanaka Beretanee"—men of Britain.

Vancouver gave Kamehameha an engraved copper plate recording the event and hoisted the English flag; the ships fired a salute of eleven guns; and the cession was completed. For sixteen years Kamehameha received no word from England that the cession of his island had been accepted. He continued to consider himself a British subject, however. For in 1810, when he was ruler of all the islands in the Hawaiian chain, he wrote the following letter:

His Most Sacred Majesty George III of the United Kingdoms of Great Britain and the Sandwich Islands King, Defender of the Faith, etc., etc., etc.
Brother,
   We Kamaahamaah King of the Sandwich Islands, wishing to render every assistance to the ships of His Most Sacred Majesty's subjects who visit these seas, have sent a letter by Captain Spence, ship Duke of Portland, to His Majesty, since which Timoree [Kaumualii], King of Atooi [Kauai], has delivered his island up, and we are now in possession of the whole of the Sandwich Islands. We as subject of His Most Gracious Majesty, wish to have a seal and arms sent from Britain, so as there may be no molestation to our ships or vessels in these seas, or any hindrance whatsoever.
   Wishing Your Majesty a long, prosperous and happy reign, I am Brother
                                        Kamaahamaah
Ooahoo, Oahu, August 6th, 1810.

   This letter, probably written by John Young, brought a reply from the British foreign secretary. He promised the king that Hawaiian ships would always be respected by the Royal Navy and assured him of England's good will and protection. Kamehameha did not get the seal and coat of arms he had asked for. The British government evidently decided that an expression of friendship was as far as they wanted to go in the matter of the Sandwich Islands. But he did receive a present of two large packing cases. One was filled with brilliant new uniforms; the other contained an assortment of carpenter's tools and two ornamental brass speaking trumpets.

At last the time for Vancouver's departure from Hawaii was only a day or two away. Kamehameha was eager to spend as many of these last hours as he could with his friends. Unfortunately, a tabu period fell just at this time and forced the king to remain ashore for two nights and the intervening day. When he left the *heiau* at the conclusion of the ceremony, he learned that Vancouver planned to sail that evening with the offshore breeze. Kamehameha was quite distressed and hastened aboard the *Discovery*.

"Kanekupa," he said, "you must not go today. I did not see you all day yesterday, and today I must be ashore to see that you get all your provisions. Stay until tomorrow night. Olohana says it is a tabu day in your religion. Let us spend it together. This time you are not going to some country in this ocean, you are going back to Beretanee. We may never see each other again, my good friend."

This appeal was more than Vancouver could resist. He was deeply moved by this evidence of the king's affection and by the example of Kamehameha's generosity that came later in the day. It was a going-away present of one hundred huge hogs and as much fruit and vegetables as the ships could store.

Sunday was a day that lingered long in the memory of Hawaiians and English alike. Kamehameha and Kaahumanu, with John Young and Isaac Davis, spent the entire day on the *Discovery*. A steady parade of canoes glided between the beach and the ships. Party after party of Hawaiians climbed aboard to bid farewell to their friends from the other side of the world.

They were quiet and sad as they said good-by and murmured prayers for a safe voyage. As night fell the last group went over the side. Reluctantly they took their leave and paddled slowly to the shore.

The king and queen and the two Englishmen remained aboard until the ships actually made sail. At eight o'clock they sat down to dinner with Vancouver in the *Discovery's* cabin. Kamehameha decided that their last hours together should be jolly and gay. He assumed an air of boisterous good humor and soon had the dinner table in high spirits.

Vancouver tried to explain to the king that the earth is round and constantly turning. He had a globe brought in and pointed out Hawaii, and England on the other side. Kamehameha could not believe it.

"No, no, Kanekupa!" He laughed. "Those people would be upside down. Look. I will show you what would happen."

He placed a ship's biscuit on a plate. "The plate is the earth," he said, "and the biscuit is Hawaii."

On top of the biscuit he set a small piece of cheese. "That is Kamehameha."

Then he turned the plate over, and roared with laughter as "Hawaii" and "Kamehameha" fell to the deck.

Just before midnight an officer reported that the breeze had freshened, and Vancouver ordered the sails raised. Kamehameha was too overcome with emotion to say much. With tears in their eyes, both he and Kaahumanu touched noses with the captain in the Hawaiian manner. Then they said "Aloha" and climbed slowly down the ladder to the royal canoe.

No other white man, with the possible exceptions of Olohana and Ikake, did so much good for Kamehameha's islands as George Vancouver. He introduced valuable animals and plants: cows, sheep, and goats; oranges, grapes, and many garden vegetables. He gave the king a variety of carpenter's and blacksmith's tools and many household utensils, and taught his people the art of shipbuilding.

While he was not immediately successful in discouraging warfare in the islands, his arguments in favor of peace undoubtedly had a strong influence later. And most of all, by his generous and sympathetic friendliness Vancouver assured all later visitors of a warm welcome from the Hawaiian king.

CHAPTER 14

Human Cataract

SHORTLY AFTER Vancouver left the islands, Kamehameha received exciting news. His ancient enemy, Kahekili, had died on Oahu. The Thunderer had lived many long years, and he had let few of them pass without making himself the most dangerous threat to the kings of Hawaii. He had fought off Kalaniopuu during the whole of that monarch's reign, and for the last twelve years he had been a formidable opponent to Kamehameha.

The news of Kahekili's death was brought by two passing ships that sent ashore a boat with a letter for John Young. Kahekili's son, Kalanikupule, had declared himself king of Maui, Molokai, Lanai, and Oahu. But, the letter said, many of the chiefs were opposed to his rule.

Kamehameha had long ago begun making preparations for just such a chance. Sixteen thousand warriors were trained and ready, and a huge fleet of double canoes was standing by to carry them across the channels from island to island. Led by the new schooner *Britannia,* which was fitted with brass cannon from the *Fair American,* it was the most powerful striking force ever assembled up to that time in any of the Pacific Islands.

Within a week the armada was on its way to Maui. This was to be Kamehameha's supreme bid for power, the effort upon which his whole future would depend. To impress upon his warriors that there could be no such thing as failure, he ordered them to take apart the double canoes and bury them in the sand of the Maui beaches.

Then he shouted a stirring battle cry:

"Forward! Forward, my brothers! To retreat is death!"

But all these preparations turned out to be unnecessary. Maui collapsed like a rotten melon. Molokai and Lanai fell just as easily.

Now Kamehameha was back where he had been five years ago after the battle of "The Damming of the Waters." Had Kanekupa been right, that anyone could take these middle islands but no one could hold them? Not this time, resolved Kamehameha. This conquest would be complete.

It was evident that the showdown with Kalanikupule was to be on Oahu. Kamehameha moved on from Molokai without pausing any longer than was necessary to prepare his fleet for the landing. The Oahuans might choose to fight in the coral-floored surf, or they might wait to defend specially prepared positions inland. This last was Kamehameha's guess, but he was ready to fight for a beachhead if necessary.

On the foredeck of the *Britannia,* Kamehameha stood in full view among his chiefs, tall and terrible in his crested helmet and golden battle cloak. Beside him a *kahuna* bore the grinning shark-toothed war god, Kukailimoku. Grouped about the flagship was a formation of hundreds of war canoes. The platforms of the great *peleleus* were loaded with warriors, and their sails, like enormous lobster claws, grasped at the sky.

The Hawaiian fleet swept up to Oahu in an immense crescent that extended for three miles on either side of Diamond Head. Their paddles churned the sea white as the canoes came in through the pale green shallows and disgorged their thousands of gourd-helmeted warriors. Kamehameha's guess had been right. The beaches were empty.

Kalanikupule had decided not to oppose the landing. He preferred a battlefield in the interior of the island. If he had feared an immediate attack, he was pleasantly surprised. For several weeks the army of Oahu had to meet nothing more formidable than skirmishing advance patrols.

Kamehameha was moving carefully. Perhaps one fierce onslaught would make him master of Oahu. Perhaps, on the other hand, it would take a long campaign. He was not going to let his quick victories on the other islands lead him to make a rash move here.

He set up his headquarters in the Waikiki coconut grove that had been the country estate of old Kahekili. Then he put his men to planting fields of taro and sweet potatoes to ensure a food supply in case the war should drag out. He knew that an army fights on its stomach.

It was at this time that Kamehameha suffered the only serious desertion of his career. The disloyal Kaiana finally came out in his true colors and went over to the Oahu army with a small band of his personal followers. His treason was no great surprise to Kamehameha. For a long time the reputation of the handsome chief had been steadily falling among the Hawaiian nobles. His haughty manner and constant discontent had left him few friends. Now he had probably decided that his best move was to try a change of masters.

When Kamehameha heard of Kaiana's desertion his only comment was, "Good. I put up with the troublemaker too long, anyway. Now I can treat him as an enemy."

Early in April 1795, Kamehameha was ready to take the offensive. He ordered his *kahunas* to make the customary auguries to determine whether the gods were agreeable. The omens were favorable. All signs pointed to victory.

Kalanikupule had built his defenses in the Nuuanu Valley that rises from the plain where Honolulu now stands up into the island's backbone of mountains. It seemed to him a good position, protected along the sides by steep, slippery walls of rock. The attackers would be forced to fight an uphill battle. If the defenders had to retreat, their front would be constantly shortened by the narrowing of the valley.

Kamehameha launched his attack on a bright spring morning. A fine mist of "liquid sunshine" blew down from the clouds wreathing the distant mountain peaks. It helped to put down the great cloud of dust raised by the marching men. Across the plain toward the first of Kalanikupule's stone barriers surged the Hawaiian host, a strange mixture of the primitive and the modern.

Most of the warriors were armed with the weapons of their ancestors. First came the companies of fighters who would engage the enemy at long range. Slingers, with their hair and fiber slings held across their backs ready to send the round stones low and level to the target. Spearmen, bearing heavy sixteen-foot shafts or shorter javelins, polished and pointed, or barbed with sharks' teeth. Then followed the great mass of hand-to-hand fighters armed with knobbed war clubs and lava-headed battle axes. Some carried cords for strangling, and wicked knives sharpened at both ends with the handle in the middle.

In addition to these ancient weapons, there was a liberal sprinkling of foreign muskets. And most deadly of all, a battery of cannon commanded by John Young and Isaac Davis. The rank and file of the army wore only tapa loincloths and gourd helmets, with perhaps a *lauhala* mat for protection. But dotting the mass of glistening brown bodies were bright spots of color, the gaudy feather helmets and capes of the chiefs.

Before the actual fighting began, the two armies indulged in a traditional Polynesian ceremony. When Kamehameha's men were within earshot of the barricade, *kahunas* from both sides ran out into the space between the lines. They bore images of their war gods and began to shout taunts and jeers back and forth.

Bitter invective and personal insults directed against the opposing chiefs filled the air. And all the while they screamed their abuse, the *kahunas* made fierce gestures at one another. They stuck out their tongues and contorted their faces into all sorts of insulting grimaces.

In this battle, for the first time, Kamehameha adopted a principle of foreign generalship that went strongly against his instincts. John Young had told him that no European general, far less a king, ever risked his life in front line, hand-to-hand fighting, but directed his troops from a more retired position. If he were killed, argued Olohana, the whole army would become confused and demoralized.

Kamehameha saw the point. But he was determined to do at least one thing in the old way—he would strike the first blow. Striding out in front of his warriors, he hurled a polished spear at the Oahu lines, and the battle was on.

The fighting was vicious. Soon the lower slope of the valley was sprinkled with the dead. Here and there were clusters of bodies where Kamehameha's cannon had sent their iron balls plowing into the Oahu ranks. And then, early in the battle, something happened that gave the Hawaiians an unexpected psychological advantage.

Kamehameha spied the deserter Kaiana, yelling taunts and handling a musket like an expert. The king went over to where John Young was sweating at his gun.

"Olohana," he shouted, pointing, "there is a good target for your cannon. Put an end to the traitor's insults."

Olohana aimed his gun carefully and touched it off. Kaiana toppled over dead.

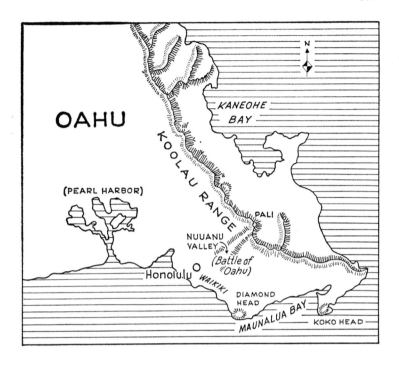

The Oahuans had already begun to retreat from their defenses. When they saw Kaiana fall they became panic-stricken. They fled up the valley with Kamehameha's warriors close behind, while Young and Davis moved their guns ever forward to new positions. From time to time the men of Oahu rallied and fought bravely in sheer desperation. But the valley only compressed them into a better target for the relentless gunners. Soon all was over but the terrible last act.

The Nuuanu Valley rises steadily, becoming narrower and

narrower, until it ends at the Pali, a V-shaped cleft in the top of the ridge. Through this gap the trade winds blow in a steady, powerful rush of air. On the windward side of the Pali the mountain drops straight down for a thousand feet in a vertical wall of black rock.

The enemy who remained alive, several hundred of them, were packed in a dense mass at the very top of the Pali. There was scarcely room for them to use their weapons. Shouting triumphantly, Kamehameha's warriors charged forward with their long spears and literally pushed the remnant of Kalanikupule's army over the precipice.

Over and over the Oahuans turned as they hurtled down, a cataract of screaming brown against the black face of the cliff, to be dashed to death on the rocks a thousand feet below.

Some few lucky ones managed to escape up the steep walls of the valley. Kalanikupule was among them, but he was captured after weeks of miserable wandering in the forest. He became the last sacrifice on the altar of Kukailimoku.

A few days after the battle, Kamehameha was sitting in state in a pleasant grove at Waikiki. About him were grouped the highest chiefs of Hawaii and the *kahunas* with the images of the gods. The new master of Oahu was holding a *hookapu*. At this feudal ceremony the principal men of the conquered island would come forward and acknowledge Kamehameha as their sovereign. This was done by presenting the conquerer with a gift to symbolize the giver's submission and fealty.

One by one the chiefs who had survived the slaughter advanced with their offerings and prostrated themselves at Kamehameha's feet. The pile of gifts grew steadily. There were priceless feather cloaks, bundles of beautifully decorated tapa cloth, finely woven *lauhala* mats, polished spears and javelins, and shining surfboards, carefully carved and oiled.

Among the last to come forward was a white-haired chief of Oahu, too old to have taken part in the fighting. He bore no gift, but he led by the hand a girl about eighteen years old. She wore a skirt of yellow tapa cloth, and a bright yellow hibiscus flower in her gleaming dark hair. Walking beside the old man, with her eyes cast down, she approached Kamehameha. The pair bowed before the king.

"O mighty one," said the aged chief, "I bring you as my token of submission and loyalty my most precious possession. This is my youngest daughter. If you will look on her with favor, she is yours."

"What is her name?" asked the king.

"Leilehua," the father answered, "The Bright Lehua Blossom."

Kamehameha spoke to the girl. "Lift your head, Leilehua, that we may see your face."

She looked up at him then, and the chiefs exclaimed in admiration at her beauty and sweet innocence.

"You are well named," said the king gently. "Come forward and give me your hand."

But instead of advancing to receive this great honor, the girl fell upon her knees and burst into tears.

Suddenly a tall youth stepped forward from the group of

Hawaiian warriors. He strode up to the kneeling girl and raised her to her feet. Then with his arm about her shoulders, he faced the king defiantly.

Kamehameha's face clouded with anger. The onlookers gasped in astonishment, and some of the nearest courtiers laid their hands on their knives. Kamehameha stopped them with a gesture and addressed the young soldier by name.

"Hakuole," he said, his voice vibrant with displeasure, "you know the penalty for laying hands on what belongs to your king. What makes you court death so boldly?"

Hakuole did not take his arm from around the trembling girl.

"Your Majesty," he replied, "I love her."

"You love her? Why, she is an Oahu girl, and you have never been here before. How can you love her?"

Hakuole answered without fear.

"I met her here at Waikiki, O king, while we were preparing for the battle. She had come down to the beach for water with her young brother. He was diving to fill his gourds at a fresh spring that flows from under the ledge of coral. Leilehua and I knew immediately that we loved each other, and she agreed to sail back to Hawaii with me. And now her father would give her away like a piece of tapa."

He stopped then, as though just realizing what a rash thing he had done.

"I see you are tired of being a soldier," said Kamehameha.

During the young man's speech the angry frown had gradually faded from the king's face, but Hakuole was now too frightened to notice.

"No, your Majesty," he stammered. "I would fight for you always. But if Leilehua cannot be my wife, I do not care to live."

Turning to the girl, Kamehameha asked, "Do you love this young hothead who dares to challenge the king himself?"

"Yes, your Majesty," she replied.

"Then here is my sentence," announced Kamehameha. "Leilehua, tonight you shall be married to him. Hakuole, I release you from military service for thirteen months. Go with her to her father's estate and see that you make her a good husband."

Then Kamehameha addressed the crowd that surrounded him: "Tonight let us feast together and dance and forget the killing that has been done. Let the marriage of these children be a symbol of the union of the people of Oahu with the people of Hawaii—my people, all of you."

CHAPTER 15

Yankee Skippers and Scented Wood

By his overwhelming victory at the Nuuana Pali, Kamehameha had made himself king of all the islands of the chain except the two most westerly ones, Kauai and its little satellite Niihau. It should be an easy task to add those to his realm, he thought, and complete the union of the whole Hawaiian group. When things had settled down on Oahu, he would go over to Kauai and have it out with Kaumualii, the chief who had set himself up as king.

In the spring of 1796 Kamehameha once more assembled his war fleet, this time on the western Oahu beaches at Waianae, and began the eighty-mile crossing to Kauai. The gods of the winds and the clouds fought against him, for, when the fleet was in the middle of the channel, a surprise storm lashed the sea into sudden fury. Canoes were swamped by the huge waves, hundreds of warriors were drowned, and the remnant of the expedition was forced to turn back to Oahu.

It was a staggering blow, but Kamehameha accepted it with resignation. Evidently the gods were not yet ready to watch him round out the empire on which his heart had been set for so long.

At Honolulu he found news waiting that sent him hurrying down to Hawaii. A brother of the traitor Kaiana had stirred up a revolt among some disgruntled chiefs. It proved to be a small-scale affair and was soon put down. But the fact that it should happen at all turned Kamehameha's attention to the administrative machinery of his new realm.

The entire system of government needed to be overhauled. Now he had not a single, compact island to rule, but an overseas empire. The problem was quite different. Kauai could wait; for all practical purposes it was as good as conquered. Once the other islands were properly administered, Kaumualii could never hope to oppose the will of his powerful neighbor.

And so for the next six years Kamehameha turned from war. He devoted all his energies to two activities of a peaceful nature: the internal improvement of his empire, and his dealings with the ever-growing number of foreign merchantmen.

It seemed to Kamehameha that the most effective way of controlling his realm was by a strong central government, he being the center—or rather, he and Kaahumanu. He created a new title of *kuhina nui*, or premier, for his capable and strong-minded favorite queen. The office was continued for nearly three quarters of a century in the Hawaiian kingdom and carried great power. Kaahumanu was set up as a sort of special counselor with the power of life and death, condemnation and acquittal, over her subjects. She had the right to veto public acts of the king himself.

Kamehameha claimed all the lands as his own by right of conquest. The faithful chiefs who had helped him to the throne and had followed him through all his campaigns were given large estates divided among the various islands. The old island kings were replaced by governors who exercised extensive local power. Old Keeaumoku, "the kingmaker," was appointed governor of Maui. One of Kaahumanu's brothers, who had named himself "John Adams" after the President of the United States, was made governor of the Kona district on Hawaii.

It was to John Young that Kamehameha entrusted the most important posts. He left Olohana in charge on Oahu after the conquest, and made him governor of the entire island of Hawaii from 1802 to 1812, a period when the royal court was located at Honolulu.

One of the most enlightened of Kamehameha's policies was his humane treatment of the conquered nobility of the central islands. He was a ruthless enemy, but a merciful and generous victor. Custom required, of course, that a principal adversary like Kalanikupule should be sacrificed to the war god. But the other numerous relatives of King Kahekili were permitted to retain large estates and continue to live as chiefs.

The lesser chiefs, whose loyalty was not so firmly established, were gathered about the king to form his court. There he could keep his eye on them and forestall any more incidents like the revolt of Kaiana's brother. He took this retinue with him everywhere, even fishing.

Kamehameha was an ardent fisherman. Whenever he heard the sport was good at some particular place, he would pack up his court and be off for a few days. Not all his courtiers were as willing as he was to put up with the discomforts of these trips. When they complained, Kamehameha would say, "I am not a straw better off than you are. If I let you remain on your estates you would become as fat as your hogs and have no other thoughts than how to make trouble for your king."

This reorganizing of his government seated Kamehameha solidly on the throne of his Pacific empire. He was certainly an absolute monarch. But he was a benevolent one, too, whose first concern always was the well-being of his beloved islands.

When Kamehameha turned his attention from politics to the condition of his land, he found there was a great deal to be done. The ravages of war that had distressed Vancouver were evident everywhere. These were due not only to the actual destruction where raids and battles had taken place but also to the fact that for many years the people had been forced to devote a large part of their time and energy to military training and preparations. And the land showed it. On every one of the islands there were overgrown trails, clogged irrigation ditches, and fields fallen into neglect.

Now that the islands could look forward to an era of peace, Kamehameha started an active program of rehabilitation. He urged his people to live close to the soil and develop their farms and fisheries, making use of the improved tools and methods introduced by the foreigners. He set the example himself by working in the royal taro patch and carrying stones to build fish ponds in the coastal shallows. And he distributed among the islands the offspring of Vancouver's cattle and sheep and goats that had multiplied wonderfully during the tabu period.

In addition to setting his domestic affairs in order, Kamehameha found that he had to devote more and more time to his relations with the outside world. Within a dozen years after Captain Cook's death, American and English merchantmen were sailing the Pacific in large numbers. By 1800 Russian fur and fishing enterprises were firmly established in Alaska and the Aleutian Islands.

In the center of all this activity lay Kamehameha's kingdom. Those volcanos that had pushed up through the ocean so many ages ago had chosen the perfect spot to be the crossroads of the North Pacific. What could be more welcome to weary sailors, after months of cruising along the bleak coasts of the fur country, than a stopover at those warm and friendly islands? There they could thaw out and stock up with supplies for the galley—hogs, chickens, sweet potatoes, fresh water, firewood.

At first Kamehameha and his chiefs had been willing to supply all these things for cheap trinkets and knicknacks. It was John Young who taught them the real value of the goods they sent out to the foreign ships. He taught them to demand tools, household implements, cloth, firearms, ammunition, and even ships and naval stores.

About ten years before the turn of the century, Kamehameha found that his islands had another commodity besides food to sell to the traders. In the mountain forests grew a variety of tree that the Hawaiians had never considered especially different from any other. But one day an American sea captain who had been to China saw a piece of the wood and eagerly offered to buy all that Kamehameha's people could lay their hands on. It was the fragrant sandalwood that ships from the East Indies sold for over one hundred dollars a ton at Canton. The Chinese prized it highly for making boxes, images, and inlay work, and they distilled the oil from the heartwood to make incense.

Word of this new way to wealth soon spread among the sea captains, and each year found more of them clamoring for a load of the precious wood. New England skippers were especially active, and John Jacob Astor added sandalwood to his fur enterprises.

While the supply of sandalwood lasted, the Hawaiian nobles accumulated enormous wealth in money or in the luxury products of China. They piled up silks and expensive inlaid furniture far beyond their needs, so that they had to build stone warehouses to store it. They bought foreign ships, the usual price being twice the amount of wood the vessel would hold.

In 1817 Kamehameha sent one of these ships, renamed the *Kaahumanu,* to China with a load of sandalwood. He lost money on the venture because of mismanagement on the part of the captain, but he profited in another way.

The account book showed a heavy charge for pilot service in and out of Chinese harbors. What was all that about? The captain explained that it was customary all over the world. Well, decided the king, he could play at that game, too. Thereafter, he required all ships entering or leaving Honolulu harbor to take aboard a pilot and pay a fee into the treasury.

Sandalwood brought wealth to the nobles, but to the common people it brought as great misery as the constant warfare of the old days. They were still serfs, subject to the labor demands of their overlords. And now the only labor their overlords thought it worth while to demand was collection of the fragrant wood.

Men and women were taken from their farms and sent up into the mountain forests to fell the trees and haul the wood down to the coast. Fields and fishing grounds were deserted, and the islands were threatened with famine. The workers prayed for the day when there would be no more of the hated trees left. Many of them hastened that time by pulling up every sandalwood sapling they found.

Kamehameha saw the suffering of the people and the waste of this valuable national resource, but he seems to have been powerless against the greed of the chiefs. Let us make hay while we can, was their motto. They paid no attention to the king's warnings, and by 1825 hardly one of the precious trees was to be found in the islands.

Kamehameha became known among the sailing captains as a good businessman. He was shrewd and well versed in all the tricks of the trade, but at the same time he was honest. So successful was he that when he died he left a treasure of nearly half a million dollars, as well as several ships and a great store of merchandise.

His fair and upright methods of dealing were illustrated when an English ship ran aground off Oahu. To refloat her, the crew had to throw overboard ninety ingots of copper. Kamehameha sent divers down to bring the copper to the beach. He then asked what part of a cargo salvagers received in Europe. When he was told one-eighth, he would take only eleven ingots, although he might have kept them all.

If Kamehameha was fair in his trading with foreigners, he was also quick to resent any sharp practice on their part. A Captain Barber offered some rum for sale and gave the king a sample bottle. When his purchase arrived, Kamehameha thought the liquor looked pale and compared it with the sample.

"They are different," he said. "This Barber shows one thing and sells another." And he sent the rum back to the ship, telling Barber that he would buy nothing more from him.

Sometime later this same ship went on the rocks off what is now called Barbers Point, near Pearl Harbor, and the wreck was looted. The captain made a hot, dusty journey to the king to complain. When he arrived, he was thirsty and asked for a drink.

"Certainly, Barber," said Kamehameha, pouring him a glass of water. "Here is some of your favorite kind of rum."

The king showed that he had not forgotten, but he saw to it that the stolen goods were returned.

CHAPTER 16

Tabu in a Frock Coat

IN 1804 THE ISLANDS of Kauai and Niihau were still nominally independent of the Hawaiian empire. For six years Kamehameha had left them in peace, but he had by no means forgotten them. The union of the islands, his life's ambition, was incomplete so long as those two remained outside the pale. It was not merely a matter of personal pride with Kamehameha; he sincerely believed in the necessity for a united Hawaii.

For this reason he sent the king of Kauai an ultimatum: acknowledge dependency or be invaded. When Kaumualii made no reply, Kamehameha began to assemble a fleet of war canoes and armed schooners. He moved slowly and regretfully, for he had become used to the ways of peace and found them pleasant.

It turned out, however, that the peace was not to be broken. Just as the army was ready to embark, a plague broke out in the camp on Oahu. The exact nature of the disease was never determined—it was most likely cholera brought by a foreign ship—but it spread like wildfire among the warriors. Kamehameha himself fell ill. When he recovered, it was to find that half his army had been wiped out. For the second time the gods had interposed to prevent his taking Kauai. Kamehameha sent another envoy to Kaumualii. If the king would agree to bring his island into the Hawaiian empire, he would be allowed to continue as the local ruler. Realizing that ultimately he would be defeated, Kaumualii was willing to accept the proposal. But Kamehameha insisted that he come to Oahu and make the submission in person. This the Kauai king was rather reluctant to do. He recalled how Keoua of the Scarlet Cloak had been greeted on a similar occasion. And so the affair dragged on for half a dozen years.

After the disaster of the plague, Kamehameha continued to live on Oahu until 1812. He left Hawaii under the governorship of John Young and moved his court first to Waikiki and later to Honolulu.

The future capital of the islands was growing fast. A year after its discovery by Captain Brown in 1794, Honolulu harbor was surveyed by a British naval vessel and added to the charts of the merchant skippers. Its sheltering reef made it far the best anchorage in the islands and it soon became a more popular stopping place than Kealakekua or the other bays. But not until after Kamehameha's death was the royal court moved permanently to Oahu.

Kamehameha's Honolulu palace stood close to the shore in

the shade of a grove of tall coconut trees. It was not all under one roof, but was really a small settlement of grass buildings surrounded by a palisade. There was the king's living and eating house, his sleeping house, the queen's house, a guard house, a powder magazine, several huts for the servants, and two solidly built stone warehouses crammed like auction rooms with the king's precious European and Chinese goods. From the palace Kamehameha could look out at the powerful little navy he had built to protect his island empire. Hauled up on the shore at Waikiki were thirty small European-type vessels. Their spars were secured alongside them and their rigging and cables stored in warehouses. In the harbor at Honolulu were a dozen more, the largest being the *Leila Byrd*—popularly known as the *Lilly Bird*—a two-hundred-ton American ship that the king had bought and made the flagship of his navy. A small sloop made regular trips between Oahu and Hawaii.

The everyday mode of life at the palace was extremely simple and well regulated. Breakfast was at eight, dinner at noon, and supper at sunset. Twenty or thirty chiefs and visitors usually sat down with the king on the *lauhala* mats spread on the eating house floor. Everything was scrupulously clean, as was true of old Hawaiian homes in general. The menu seldom varied: poi, with fish and pork that had been consecrated at the *heiau*.

Kamehameha liked to finish off his dinner with half a glass of rum—half a glass and no more. When rum was introduced into Hawaii about 1791 he had been quite partial to it. He tried it first aboard a foreign ship at Kailua and came ashore staggering. Seeing him in this state, the people set up a cry of despair.

"A-we! A-we! Kamehameha has become crazy!"

"No," said the chiefs who had been on the ship with him. "The foreigners say he will be all right. They have a water that causes men's knees to go loose."

Here again the good sense and solicitude of John Young had served Kamehameha well. Olohana, who was a sober-minded man and wrote religious verse, persuaded the king to be moderate in his drinking. It is said that Kamehameha felt so strongly on the subject toward the end of his life that he forbade the making of liquor and ordered all the stills destroyed.

The first stills on the islands were operated by six or seven escaped convicts from the Australian penal colony at Botany Bay. One of them rigged up a contraption with gun barrels and an iron kettle and distilled liquor from the root of the ti plant. The Hawaiians took a taste and named it *okole-hao* ("iron-bottom"), referring either to the iron pot or to the sort of stomach a man must have to drink the stuff.

These same convicts managed to gather about themselves at Honolulu a crew of lively ne'er-do-wells who held carouses far into the night. It was not an unusual thing for them to open a keg of rum and sit around it for days until they had emptied it.

Kamehameha had his own characteristic way of dealing with them. After one particularly riotous disturbance a messenger informed them that the next time they started a brawl the king himself would come over and take part in it and see who should be the last man left standing. Drunken riots immediately became less popular.

Although Kamehameha would not put up with brawling, his love of sports and games and entertainments stayed with him throughout his life, and so did his sense of humor. In common with all Hawaiians, he thought the European style of dancing together very funny. He would rock with laughter watching a pair of the court comics give a ridiculous imitation of the waltz.

His favorite game in his old age was *konane,* a complicated form of checkers played with black and white pebbles. The king was an expert and would sit at the board with his chiefs for hours at a time, smiling when he made a good move but never uttering a syllable.

But Kamehameha was no mere armchair athlete. Until the year he died he maintained his reputation as one of the best surfboard riders in the islands. And when horses were introduced into Hawaii in 1803, the fifty-year-old king was one of the first to learn to ride.

When Kamehameha walked about the streets of Honolulu, he was always attended by three servants. One waved a feather fly chaser, one carried the royal spitbox, and the third stood by in case the king should wish to take off his clothes. For while in most things he was faithful to the ways of his ancestors, Kamehameha did enjoy wearing European clothes. He would often start out in the morning dressed in a shirt, a black frock coat, and trousers. But soon exercise and the mounting sun had him perspiring and pulling at his collar. Then, wherever he might be, the king would take off the so-called civilized garments, hand them to the waiting servant, and be on his way clad only in his more comfortable malo.

Although he was willing to give the white man's clothes a try, Kamehameha made no compromise when it came to observing the ancient religious laws of his people. He spent two nights and the intervening day of each week at the *heiau* in prayer and meditation. Every year he opened the *makahiki* festival by actually risking his life to prove to his people in the traditional manner that he was still a man worthy of being their king. Before he went to the *heiau*, three warriors, one after the other, hurled their spears at him. He caught the first and used it to ward off the other two.

When a foreign visitor remarked on the personal danger involved, the king answered, "There is no danger. There is no man in Hawaii who can throw the spear that I cannot catch."

Kamehameha never changed his belief that "the life of the land," as he put it, depended on strict observance of the sacred tabus. The foreigners, of course, ignored them, and the younger generation of Hawaiians came to disbelieve in the power of the ancient gods. But as long as Kamehameha lived, the punishment for violating a tabu, intentionally or not, was swift and savage.

One day Archibald Campbell, the king's Scottish sailmaker, saw the body of a woman rolling about unnoticed in the Waikiki surf. She had got drunk, he was told, and had entered the eating house of men. For the latter offense she had been strangled and thrown into the sea.

On another occasion a foreigner ventured to ask the king
why one man had been put to death for eating a coconut during a tabu period, while another had gone unpunished after
killing his small son in a fit of rage. "The man who killed his son," explained Kamehameha,
"harmed no one but himself. The man who broke the tabu
hurt all Hawaii in the estimation of the gods."

There was a marked contrast between the simple routine of
Kamehameha's daily life and the time-honored tributes of respect that were paid to the king's person and to everything he
used. Whenever the king passed by, his subjects were required
to uncover their heads and shoulders. They rendered the same
salute when they passed the royal residence, or even any building that the king had ever entered.

Once, when Campbell was working on his sails in Isaac Davis' house, he saw Kamehameha passing by. He stepped to the
door and asked the king to come in and see his work. Kamehameha declined, explaining the custom, but sat at the door while
Campbell brought out samples of the cloth.

When the servants carried Kamehameha's food to his eating
house they called out, "*Noho! Noho!* ("Sit down! Sit down!").
Then everyone within hearing had to uncover himself and
squat on the ground. This ceremony was especially inconveni-
ent when the royal drinking water was being carried to the
palace. The water at Honolulu was rather brackish, so the
king's was brought in calabashes from springs five miles up the
Manoa valley. When the bearers met anyone in their long journey they were required to shout the "*Noho!*" warning, but

they ran past the squatters quickly so as to cause a minimum of discomfort.

It must not be imagined from all this that Kamehameha was a heartless despot who gave no thought to the personal comfort of his subjects. On the contrary, when Archibald Campbell announced that he was going back to England, Kamehameha asked the sailor to be sure to present his compliments to King George.

"King George?" exclaimed Campbell. "Why I never saw him in my life, and I'm not likely to when I get back. I have never even been in the same city where he lives, and neither have thousands of other Englishmen."

Kamehameha was visibly surprised.

"But does he not travel about among his people, as I do, to learn their wants?"

"No. He has other people who do that for him."

"That is not a good way," objected the king. "I know that nobody else could do it for me as well as I can myself."

The quarrel over the cession of Kauai continued to smolder, but with each passing year it came nearer to bursting into flame. Kaumualii maintained his stubborn refusal to cede the island in person, and Kamehameha became more and more angry. Foreign sea captains, who were fearful that war would interrupt the profitable sandalwood trade, did their best to bring the two kings together.

Finally, in the summer of 1810, an American, Captain Winship, persuaded Kaumualii to go with him to Oahu. Kamehameha had a salute fired when the ship entered the harbor and went out in a canoe to meet it.

When he climbed over the side, the Kauai king said to him, "Here I am. Is it face up or face down?"

Kamehameha replied, "There is no death."

"Here is my tribute in coming to this conference," said Kaumualii, pointing to his chiefs. "The government of Kauai, the chiefs and the common people, high and low, all are yours."

"I will not take away your authority or any part of your lands," announced Kamehameha generously. "When you go home, keep your power. But it is my wish that my chiefs may visit your island and be received courteously."

"Now," said a *kahuna* who was present, "the protecting cloud of Kamehameha rests on the mountain tops of all the islands."

CHAPTER 17

New Flag in the Breeze

Now THAT HE WAS ruler of an empire that stretched across five hundred miles of the Pacific Ocean, Kamehameha felt he should have a flag of his own. Ever since 1794 he had used the English flag given to him by George Vancouver. But now he wanted something more distinctive. He wanted a flag that would indicate his attachment to Britain and at the same time symbolize Hawaii.

The queens and the chiefs suggested all sorts of colorful designs, but Kamehameha's choice was a beautiful arrangement worked out by George Beckley, a sea captain who had settled on Oahu in 1806. Beckley seems to have been inspired by the pattern of the Stars and Stripes. In the upper quarter next to the staff he set the Union Jack. The rest of the flag he filled with eight broad horizontal stripes alternating white, red, and blue, one for each of the islands over which the banner was to wave for the next ninety years.

Shortly after adoption of the new flag, the War of 1812

brought Hawaii its first visit by a United States naval vessel. The war did not touch the Hawaiian Islands in any spectacular way. No important naval engagements were fought in the island waters, and King Kamehameha was never called upon to demonstrate his loyalty to King George. For a year or two he noticed a falling off in the number of merchant ships that called and a decline in the profits from the sandalwood trade.

The first visiting ship to represent the United States Navy was only temporarily American, but it flew the Stars and Stripes long enough to be the precursor of the great fleets that would one day jam Pearl Harbor. It was the *Sir Andrew Hammond,* an armed whaling ship captured from the British and commanded by Lieutenant John Gamble of the United States Marine Corps.

Lieutenant Gamble had been left at Nukuheva, in the Marquesas Islands, in charge of three English whalers taken by Captain David Porter. But his stay there had been a discouraging series of misfortunes. The natives killed several of his men. Then the English prisoners staged a mutiny and recaptured one of the ships. Gamble decided to burn one of the remaining whalers and sail the *Sir Andrew Hammond* to the Hawaiian Islands for supplies. He anchored for several days in Waikiki Bay and then set sail for the island of Hawaii.

His streak of bad luck continued. Off the coast of Maui, Gamble's ship was captured by a British sloop-of-war, the *Cherub,* which was also on its way to Hawaii.

One of the days Lieutenant Gamble was aboard the *Cherub* happened to be the Fourth of July, 1814, and this was the occasion of an inspiring example of courtesy among enemies. The ship's captain ordered a special dinner with extra wine to be served in the wardroom, and the lieutenant and another captured American officer were able to celebrate the holiday in spite of being prisoners on an English warship.

When the *Cherub* reached Hawaii, its commander sent Kamehameha an invitation to have dinner on board. The king was accompanied by Olohana and four of the royal wives. Each of the women, according to Lieutenant Gamble's astonished estimate, weighed over three hundred pounds.

The most human and sympathetic account of Kamehameha in the last years of his life was written by Lieutenant Otto von Kotzebue commanding the ship *Rurick* of the Russian navy. On its way home from a cruise to the coast of California the *Rurick* dropped anchor off Kailua on Hawaii in the fall of 1816.

When Kotzebue arrived, Kamehameha and his court were camping out some distance down the coast on an extremely hot stretch of bare lava rock. The king was amusing himself. He had heard that the bonito were running and, as was his custom, he had moved his court, bag and baggage, to the fishing ground.

As soon as he heard of the ship's arrival, Kamehameha hurried back to Kailua with his chiefs. Dressed in a white shirt, blue trousers, red waistcoat, and a yellow silk neckcloth, he received his visitor at the palace and at once showed his generous nature.

"I understand," he said to Kotzebue through an interpreter, "that you are an explorer like Cook and Vancouver and that you do not engage in commerce. I will not treat you as a trader, therefore, but will provide you with whatever you need that my islands produce.

"Since Kamehameha has been king of these islands," he continued, "no European has had cause to complain of being treated unjustly here. I have made my islands a haven for all nations, and have honestly supplied with provisions every ship that has desired them."

Kamehameha invited Kotzebue and his officers to a banquet that evening. Everything was most elaborate and in the European style. The guests sat at an imported mahogany table on imported chairs and drank imported wine. Each of the Russians had an attendant who kept his glass full and plied him with an endless succession of dishes: pork, beef—descendants of Vancouver's cows—fowl, and choice island vegetables and fruits.

Kamehameha and his chiefs sat at the table but did not eat because the food had not been properly consecrated. The king astonished his visitor with his knowledge of happenings and conditions in the outside world and his keen questions about Russian affairs. He was in high good humor, and although much of his wit was lost on his guests, the chiefs were constantly laughing at his remarks.

After healths had been drunk all around, Kamehameha gave a feather lei to Kotzebue and said, "I have heard that your emperor is a great hero. I love him for it, for I am one myself. Take him this lei as a token of my regard."

The Russian officer replied with a formal compliment to the

king, "Your Majesty's lifelong efforts to give your people the benefits of civilization and to unite the islands have attracted the attention and admiration of the whole world."

Beaming with pleasure at this praise, the royal old warrior opened his shirt and pointed to the many battle scars on his body.

"I conquered these islands in my younger days," he said, "and these scars prove that I deserve to be king of them."

When Kotzebue and his officers had finished their dinner, Kamehameha insisted that the Russian sailors who had rowed the boats ashore be brought in and served a similar meal.

This gesture was entirely typical of the king. He always saw to it that the tabus and the privileges of the nobles were strictly observed, but in his judgment of individual men he was a true democrat. It was a man's worth and ability that counted with him. Several of his most trusted confidential advisers had been selected from the lower ranks of the social scale, and he seldom had been disappointed in his choice.

While the sailors were eating, Kamehameha took Kotzebue and his party to the *heiau* that stood near by. He led them from one to another of the grotesque wooden gods and brilliant feather-covered basketwork images that stood about the temple. One of them, hung with leis and surrounded by offerings, he embraced devoutly. Then he turned to Kotzebue and said, "These are our gods, whom I worship. Whether I do right or wrong, I don't know. But I will continue to follow my faith, which cannot be wicked as it commands me never to do evil."

Then he went alone into one of the small grass temples for a few minutes of prayer. When he came out, he invited the Russian officers to join him while he ate supper.

"I watched you while you ate a European meal," he said, "now you shall see how Kamehameha eats."

They all went to the royal eating house and sat talking with him through the meal. Kamehameha used no fork or spoon, just the eating tools he had been born with. As he twirled his fingers in a bowl of poi and carried the food to his mouth, he said, "This is the custom of my country and I will not depart from it."

It was not an apology, but an expression of pride. Evidently the knife and fork he had begged from Vancouver twenty-five years before had been just a passing fancy.

Kotzebue was strongly impressed by Kamehameha's attitude toward foreign ways and importations. Whatever he considered useful and better, he urged his people to adopt. But he did not favor a thing merely because it was new or because of a desire to ape the white man. He had European-style houses but always preferred his native grass ones. What he desired, he said, was to increase the happiness, not the wants, of his people.

Naturally the Hawaiians were attracted by the novelty of things that came from strange lands. Foreigners enjoyed great prestige in the islands, and many of their customs were imitated for that reason. In the matter of clothes, for example, the chiefs came to feel that to be formally dressed they must wear something in the foreign style. Their favorite garb for state occasions was a black frock coat and perhaps a hat—underneath, nothing but a malo. The soldiers and sentinels about the palace were naked except for a malo and a cartridge belt with pistols around the waist.

Kamehameha himself loved to dress up; in fact, he enjoyed pomp and display of any sort. He had a large wardrobe of the brilliant uniforms of the period, his favorite being that of a captain in the British navy.

Nearly everyone, Kotzebue noticed, carried a piece of looking glass and a pipe hanging around his neck on a string. Tobacco was grown on the islands, having been introduced by American traders, and smoking was an almost universal pastime. The king did not smoke, but, when Kotzebue paid a call on Kaahumanu and the other queens, he found them passing a pipe around among themselves.

Queen Kaahumanu gossiped eagerly about European affairs. She had heard that the island of St. Helena with Napoleon on it had been swallowed up by the sea. Was that true? And was it also true that George III had only one wife? What a shame that so great a king should be the husband of only one woman! She spoke with much feeling of Vancouver and his untimely death at the age of thirty-nine, and of Captain Cook, who had revealed her islands to the rest of the world when she was just a girl.

In those days before the invention of the camera, it was customary for exploring expeditions to take along an artist to make a pictorial record of the places visited. Kotzebue had with him a painter named Louis Choris. He drew several pictures of Hawaiian scenes and asked the old king to sit for his portrait. At first Kamehameha refused outright. He probably associated painting with idols and had no wish to be set up as a god. After much urging he gave in, however, and allowed Choris to paint him in the red waistcoat and yellow tie.

While the artist was at work the king was as restless as a boy. He squirmed and pulled grotesque faces as though he found it all very embarrassing. The bust-length portrait, the only one of Kamehameha in existence, shows a portly old man with short gray hair and a serious but kindly face. One can believe that thirty years earlier it had been a stern face, or even a ferocious one, but Choris shows it softened and mellowed by time.

Unfortunately, not all of the visitors to Hawaii were as friendly as Kotzebue. A year earlier, in fact, another Russian crew, led by a German adventurer named Scheffer, had attempted to build a fort at Honolulu. But they soon sailed away when John Young appeared on the scene and ordered them to leave or be driven off.

And then there were the South American pirates. These desperadoes sailed in and demanded to be supplied with food. In payment they gave gold and silver objects that were unfamiliar to the Hawaiians. One of the Europeans told Kamehameha that the treasure had come from a Catholic church and that the men must have stolen it. Before the king could take any action, a Chilean warship put in and seized the pirates' vessel, but the crew made their escape inland.

The captain of the warship explained that the men were wanted in Chile for having looted churches during the revolution. Kamehameha ordered out a troop of warriors who rounded up all the scoundrels except the leader. He was never seen or heard of again.

The majority of the foreigners in the islands, however, were law-abiding and industrious, and many of them were influenced by the generous and forceful character of the king to enter his service. Kamehameha never changed his policy of rewarding foreigners liberally if they were deserving. He gave them grants of land, not outright, but with the understanding that it could not be transferred and must be returned to the king on their death.

The most prominent of the foreigners, of course, was John Young. His friend, Isaac Davis, had died in 1810. Other Englishmen were Captain James Stewart, who helped in the conquest of Oahu, and George Beckley, who designed the Hawaiian flag. Alexander Adams, a sailor who had fought with Nelson at Trafalgar, became a pilot in Honolulu harbor; James Beattie had been on the English stage.

There were many Americans—Captain Winship, and "Homa" (Oliver Holmes) from Plymouth, Massachusetts, who had been the only white man in the service of Kalanikupule at the Pali battle. Of all the immigrants from the United States the most interesting was Anthony Allen, a runaway slave from Schenectady, New York. He married and went into business for himself near Honolulu, out toward Waikiki. Soon he was the proprietor of a prosperous little settlement: a boardinghouse for sailors, a dozen mud cottages that he rented, and a goat farm.

One of the most useful of the foreigners was a Spaniard whose full name was Don Francisco de Paula Marin—"Manini" to the Hawaiians. He made himself happy with half a dozen wives and served the king as gardener, gunsmith, and physician. He baptized two hundred Hawaiians on their deathbeds to keep them from dying heathens, and died himself in 1837 at the age of sixty-three.

CHAPTER 18

"Only the Stars . . ."

KAMEHAMEHA was lying seriously ill in his palace at Kailua on Hawaii. The news reached Honolulu when a messenger arrived in April 1819 with an urgent summons for Don Francisco to attend the king. During the winter a wave of sickness, probably some form of influenza, had swept through the Hawaiian Islands. It developed into an epidemic and took the lives of many islanders. With the coming of spring the number of deaths decreased, but the disease still lingered about. And now, the messenger said, both Kamehameha and Kaahumanu the queen had caught the illness.

When Kamehameha lived on Oahu, Manini had been the court doctor and he had a considerable knowledge of medicine. But as he hurried aboard the boat that would take him to Kailua he did not feel very confident of being able to help. Two days before the summons came, the *kahunas* at Honolulu had been worried by an unusual rise and fall of the tide. The oldest native could not remember ever before having seen the water come in so high or retreat so far as it did that day.

So uncommon an occurrence could mean only one thing—an event of major importance was about to happen in the kingdom of Hawaii.

When he reached Kailua, Manini found himself in the midst of a great gathering of *kahunas* and chiefs from all over the kingdom. The news was encouraging. Both the king and the queen were showing improvement. Kaahumanu made steady progress back toward health, and so did the king for a few days. But at the end of the month Kamehameha suffered a sudden relapse.

In desperation the priests hurriedly built a grass house near to the king's dwelling and dedicated it to a bird god that had a reputation for working miraculous cures. Kamehameha was carried there, but he grew so weak that he could no longer turn himself in bed. After three days he was taken back to his own house. Manini was unable to do anything for him.

On May 3 it was announced to the people that their king was dying. The effect of this news was a powerful tribute to Kamehameha's popularity with his subjects. Men and women abandoned their fields and homes and gathered in small groups to pray day and night for the recovery of their beloved king. None of the workaday tasks mattered any longer. All that mattered now was what was happening in the quiet grass house where the dying man lay.

Queen Kaahumanu, grief-stricken as she was, assumed the leadership of the kingdom in the emergency. Fearful that disorders might break out with the people so upset, she took the wise precaution of collecting all the muskets from the chiefs and soldiers and locking them up in the royal arsenal.

And now, as a last resort, the high priest Hewahewa proposed that they try the most awesome of all appeals to the gods—the offering of human sacrifices. It was believed in the old pagan days that, when a man died, his store of mana was liberated and passed on to the gods. They, if they were so requested by the proper prayers and ceremonies, could transfer this life-giving energy to a dying man and restore him to health.

Several of the older chiefs who still held firmly to the ancient religion instantly offered their lives to save that of their king. But Kamehameha heard the discussion from where he lay on the thick pile of soft mats.

"No!" he shouted, gathering all the strength he could muster.

With a feeble gesture he beckoned Hewahewa over to his bed.

"The lives of the people no longer belong to me," he said. "They are tabu to my successor."

For another day, and still another, the indomitable old king held on to life. Occasionally he recognized a friend by a faint smile or a slight movement of his hand on the tapa coverlet.

At ten o'clock in the evening of May 7, Kamehameha indicated that he would like something to eat. His anxious friends were pleased, for all day long they had been unable to get him to take nourishment. John Young and the high chief Hoapili ("The Faithful Comrade") lifted him up and carried him the short distance to his eating house. True to his religion to the very end, Kamehameha would not consent to take food in a house where women had been. He was able to eat only a mouthful of poi, however, and was carried back to bed.

He seemed a little brighter than before, and Kalanimoku, his prime minister, spoke to him.

"We are all here with you," he said; "your brothers, your son Liholiho, and your Englishman, Olohana. Give us your last charge."

"What do you say?" Kamehameha asked feebly.

"Your last counsel for us."

The men bending close over his couch could just make out the halting reply:

"Continue on . . . in my good way, and . . ."

He was unable to say any more, but he raised his arm and drew down John Young's head to touch noses in a last farewell. Then he motioned to Hoapili and used the last of his strength to whisper in the chief's ear his secret instructions for the disposal of his body. The chief nodded his head, and Kamehameha sank back on the mats.

He died about two o'clock in the morning on May 8, 1819, in his sixty-sixth year.

The death of any important Hawaiian was always followed by violent public exhibitions of mourning, but now the people behaved like maniacs. They threw off every restraint of conduct, as though the world were ending with the passing of their beloved king. Crowds broke into what stores of liquor they could find and ran about the streets in a drunken frenzy, shrieking and tearing off their clothes.

Men and women showed their grief by disfiguring themselves insanely. Some cut off their hair or knocked out their front teeth. Others branded circles on their faces with the small ends of heated calabashes held burning against the skin.

Liholiho, the new king, did not take part in this public mourning for his father. Custom required that he should retire from the town with his family until after the burial, for fear he might be contaminated by the presence of death.

The body of Kamehameha was carried to the *heiau* to be prepared for burial by the priests. Only the bones of the dead were preserved by the Hawaiians. The priests first washed the body and wrapped it in a shroud of green taro and banana leaves. Then they laid it in a trench and covered it with a foot of earth. Along the whole length of the trench they built a fire, which they kept burning steadily for ten days. At the end of that time the priests removed the earth and carefully separated the bones from the cooked flesh, which was later buried at sea.

That night the high chief Hoapili carried out the instructions that Kamehameha had whispered on his deathbed. Accompanied by a single faithful servant, he entered the *heiau*. He spread out a large square of black tapa, reverently laid the bones of the king on it, and wrapped them up into a compact bundle. Then he picked up the sacred burden and walked out of the *heiau*. Hoapili spoke no word of explanation, but none of the priests hindered him. They all knew that he was performing the last request of the dead king.

The streets were deserted as the two men passed through the town of Kailua and disappeared among the trees. They bore the bones of the great Hawaiian to a lonely burial cave in the face of some cliff along the Kona coast. There they rest undisturbed to this day, for neither Hoapili nor his faithful servant ever revealed the secret.

And so it was said in the islands, "Only the stars of the heavens know the resting place of Kamehameha."

Afterword

AT THE END of the mourning period Liholiho
returned to Kailua to assume the rule of the islands as Kamehameha II. He was twenty-two years old, tall like his father, but
not nearly so forceful or serious-minded. Princely and splendid
in a scarlet and gold uniform, with a yellow feather cape about
his shoulders, he appeared before a great assemblage of his
chiefs and people on the Kailua beach. He was greeted by the
dowager queen Kaahumanu.

"O royal one," she said, "listen now to the will of your
father. Behold these chiefs and these people and these lands
that were your father's. They are now yours, but it was your
father's wish that you and I rule them together."

Kaahumanu soon gave notice that she was not going to be
a silent partner in the arrangement. Six months after the
death of her husband, she successfully engineered a revolution
that abolished in one clean sweep the outmoded religion of
her forefathers.

The prohibitions of the ancient tabus were particularly ob-
noxious to the women. For several years now the court ladies
had secretly broken many of the degrading restrictions. Why,

asked Kaahumanu, should a woman not be allowed to eat pork or bananas, or take a meal in the eating house of her husband?

Practically all of the chiefs supported her: Kalanimoku, the prime minister; Keopuolani, mother of the king and of the highest ranking chief in Hawaii; and even the high priest Hewahewa. They laid their plan before Liholiho. He was not sure what the outcome would be, but he was willing to find out.

A great banquet was prepared, and all the chiefs and prominent foreigners were invited. Two tables were set in separate pavilions, one for the men and one for the women. While his guests were busily eating, the young king sent platters of the forbidden foods over to the women's table. Then he rose from his place, walked across to a seat beside Kaahumanu, and calmly began to eat.

There was a breathless, shocked silence.

But no bolt from the heavens consumed the pavilion. No furious god struck the king down.

Old Hewahewa jumped to his feet.

"The eating tabu is broken!" he shouted. "The gods are dead!" And snatching up a torch he ran off to set fire to the *heiau* with his own hands.

The next day Liholiho ordered all the tabus abolished and all the *heiaus* and idols destroyed. There was some opposition. A group of priests and conservative chiefs organized an armed revolt, but the royal forces put it down without too much difficulty. Hawaii was a land without a religion.

"What are we to worship now?" the people asked. "Are we to have not even one god to pray to?"

If they could but have known it, their answer was already on its way. For by the most happy of coincidences the brig *Thaddeus*, carrying American missionaries to the Sandwich Islands, had sailed from Boston just a week or two before Liholiho broke the tabus.

Not until they reached Hawaii did the New Englanders learn that Kamehameha had died and the pagan gods had been abolished. Then there was no doubt in the minds of those earnest ministers and their families that their enterprise was the result of divine planning.

JAMES T. POLE
Ferry Farms
Annapolis, Maryland

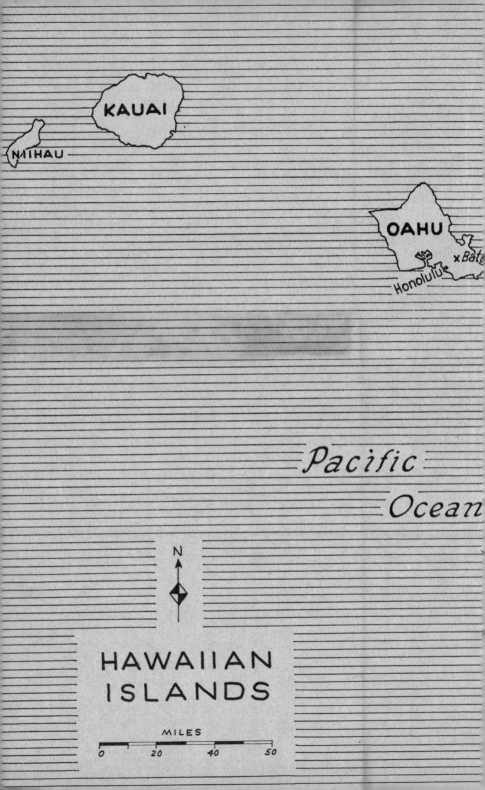